YOU ARE BORN TO BLOSSOM

Take My Journey Beyond...

Books by Dr. Kalam

You are Born to BLOSSOM

Take My Journey Beyond...

APJ Abdul Kalam

with

Arun K Tiwari

Ocean Books Pvt. Ltd.

ISO 9001:2015 Publishers

No part of this publication can be reproduced, stored in a retrieval system or transmitted in any form or by any means, electronic, mechanical, photocopying, recording or otherwise without the prior permission of the author and the publisher.

Published by
Ocean Books (P) Ltd.
4/19 Asaf Ali Road,
New Delhi-110 002 (INDIA)
e-mail: oceanbooksindia@gmail.com

ISBN 978-81-8430-336-0
YOU ARE BORN TO BLOSSOM
Take My Journey Beyond...
by Dr. APJ Abdul Kalam with Arun K Tiwari

Edition
2025

Price
₹ 350.00 (Rupees Three Hundred Fifty Only)

© Reserved

Printed at
Narula Printers, Delhi

Preface

On July 5, 2006, I visited Berhampur in South Orissa to participate in the Platinum Jubilee Celebrations of the City High School. The sight of thousands of students, who came there braving stormy weather, warmed the cockles of my heart. My friend, Kota Harinarayana, former chief of India's Light Combat Aircraft Development Programme, was with me. Kota was a distinguished alumnus of this school and I asked him, "Did you ever think, while you were a student here, that you would be developing a fighter aircraft one day?" Laughing in his characteristic manner, Kota responded, "I did not have any notion of fighter aircraft, but I was very certain that I would achieve something significant one day." Is there something latent in a child that manifests later in life?

Perhaps yes. In 1941, when my science teacher Siva Subramania Iyer, of the Rameshwaram Panchayat Board School, told me (a 10-year-old boy) that how birds fly, he indeed opened an epiphany door of perception—an explanation that eventually inspired me to fly in life, both literally and figuratively. A primary teacher carries a pivotal responsibility—that of providing a student with a complete set of precepts and practices for progress towards the essence that a child carries forward from a long genetic chain.

Having walked on this planet for three quarters of a century and having interacted with a million young students, I believe that education is indeed a complete synergetic system encompassing multiple subsystems. We can expand on the four components, which are integrated to form a connected whole, with the whole being greater than the sum of the parts. Without these four interconnected elements, no form of education will be able to lead a student to the essence that is waiting to be manifested in the life ahead. What are these elements that add up to holistic education?

The first phase comprises the practical, concrete and specific aspect of learning. The second phase involves modes and methods. It will be appropriate to say that most people manage to get to this point. It is in the third phase, that one transcends the common plane of experience and moves to a more sublime state of understanding. This phase, in essence, marks the natural progression of an evolved soul. The fourth and final stage is an expression of the philosophical and abstract dimension of human existence. The nomenclature for these four stages varies from culture to culture.

There are four stages of life in the Hindu Society, namely: *Brahmachari* (student), *Grihastha* (Householder), *Vanaprastha* (in semi-retirement) and *Sanyasi* (the renounced one in full retirement). The *Dharma* (rightful conduct) of each is different. The four stages may be said to represent periods of Preparation, Production, Service and Departure. Hinduism does not believe in an instructive doctrine. People do not have to be taught how to be happy, how to be secure or how to attain the respect and admiration of their friends and associates. Hindu thought suggests that there is a natural progression of these values and one should grow towards more fundamental interests embedded in every unique individual. This transition through natural values has been institutionalised in the understanding of the four stages of life known as *Ashrama* (abodes).

In Buddhism, the process enlightenment is explained in terms of four successive steps. These are: *Sotapanna* (a partially-enlightened person, who has eradicated the first three fetters of the mind, namely, self-view, sceptical doubt and attachment to rites and rituals); *Sakadagami* (who still has comparatively strong sensuous desires and ill-will); *Anagami* (who is completely free from sensuous desires and ill-will); and *Arahant* (a person, having removed all causes for future becoming, is not reborn after biological death into any worldly realm).

Classical Western thought spells out four stages of human spiritual development. The first stage is chaotic, disordered and reckless. One tends to defy and disobey, and is unwilling to accept a will greater than his or her own. Delinquents and mavericks are people who have never grown out of this stage. The second stage is the stage at which a person has blind faith. Once children have learnt to obey their parents, they reach this stage. Many so-called religious people are essentially second stage people, in the sense that they have blind faith in God, and do not question His existence. With blind faith come humility and a willingness to obey and serve. The majority of good law-abiding citizens never move out of the second stage. The third stage is the stage of scientific scepticism and inquisitivity. In this stage, a person will have faith in God but only after examination. People working in scientific research belong to this stage. In the fourth stage, an individual starts enjoying the mystery and beauty of Nature. While retaining scepticism, he/she starts perceiving grand patterns in Nature. Their religiousness and spirituality differ significantly from that of a second stage person, in the sense that they do not accept things through blind faith but out of genuine belief. The fourth stage people are, indeed, mystics.

In the Islamic tradition of Sufi mysticism or *Tasawwuf,* these four phases are called *Shariat, Tareeqat, Ma'refat* and *Haqeeqat,* in ascending order. *Shariat* constitutes the Rule Book or the code to be followed unambiguously. *Tareeqat* forms the training, *Ma'refat* the apparatus, so to speak, while *Haqeeqat* is the summit.

The scheme of civil society depends on educating young people to become enlightened citizens and adults who are responsible, thoughtful and enterprising. This is neither a segment of the service industry nor a work of the Government. It is, indeed, an intricate, challenging task requiring deep understanding of ethical principles, moral values, political theory, aesthetics and economics. Above all, it is an understanding of children, within them and in society. The responsibility of this task can neither be spurn away on to the Government nor can be bought off by money.

Progress in every practical field depends upon having capacities that schooling can educate. Education thus is a means to foster future development and prosperity. One's individual development and the capacity to fulfil one's own purposes can depend on an adequate preparation in childhood. The better the foundation that is built, the more successful the child will be. Simple basics in education can carry a child to greater heights.

A central tenet of education typically includes "*the imparting of knowledge*". At a very basic level, this purpose ultimately deals with the nature, origin and scope of knowledge. But equally important is to analyse the nature and variety of knowledge and how it relates to similar notions such as truth and belief. We cannot afford to educate our children on the thoughts of other nations which will, in essence, forfeit the future of our nationhood.

India has traditionally been a knowledge society. Great philosophers and scholars have walked on this land. Indian tradition captured a widespread spectrum of thoughts on the aim as well as methods of education. I found two polar positions in the writings of Rabindranath Tagore and Jiddu Krishnamurthy. Tagore said that culture is essential to nurture creativity like a garden is for the flowers to bloom. Jiddu Krishnamurthy, on the other hand, said culture destroys creativity. He sees genius as essentially a rebellion. This book takes the middle ground. Underlying the significance of traditional education that covers *Shariat* and *Tareeqat* phases which cannot be debased or flouted, the book focuses on the spirit of *Ma'refat*.

I have only written here what I have seen and felt first hand. More than five decades of work on large projects and opportunity to work under inspiring leaders, brilliant colleagues and committed juniors taught me certain things that I must share with posterity. My interpretation of *Ma'refat* is bringing about the cosmic energy into galvanising the process of manifestation of one's genetically endowed excellence. I have experienced it many times at crucial junctures of my work and I consider it as a step to progress beyond the essential.

The Indian tradition is replete with scores of such examples. The genius of Thiruvalluvar, Kabir and Vivekananda is cosmic and has transcended convention. Each, in his chosen way, in his own period, opened up new vistas of thought and reflection. Then we had a great tradition of science, particularly physics and mathematics, bringing in Noble prizes. However, today there is a trend emphasizing on acquiring service skills as compared to research. The common trend today is to follow what is laid out rather than to innovate.

The wealth in the modern world comes from innovation. The emerging field of nanotechnology is indeed open to everyone for the purpose of innovation. India can, indeed, be a world leader in this field. Information technology has brought global recognition and respect to India. However, its fruits are limited to a few hundred thousand jobs and a portion of export earnings. It must now go beyond the present scenario of providing service to innovation.

This book is an attempt to induce young minds to realise that tremendous resources and support systems exist in the field of education. These systems, however, are unseen if untried.

The book contains many 'little' ideas I found fascinating during my interaction with about a million school children over the last five years but are rarely included in conventional academics, despite being indispensable. I receive interesting questions on my website: Why do we divide a circle into 360 degrees? When were the plus and minus signs introduced into mathematics? What was all the fuss about when Copernicus discovered a thousand years later what Aryabhatta recorded in the year 499?

We live in a terror induced era. There are people who believe they will earn a honoured place in paradise by sacrificing themselves for a dream. Where does this strange notion, paradise, come from? Is not the earth an abode bestowed upon mankind? Is not every human being born destined to blossom in this very life? This book does not provide the answer. Instead of providing such answers, it asks a question—Why not? Are not all buds destined to blossom?

A.P.J. Abdul Kalam

Contents

1. The Wooing of Grain and Clay 15

2. In the Childhood Garden 33

3. The Treble of Heaven's Harmony 52

4. Living is Doing 69

5. Flowering of the Mind 86

6. Nurturing a Garden 104

Specks in Brownian Motion 117

8. Education as a Spiritual Journey 134

Epilogue 149

Endnotes 155

Acknowledgements 174

Index 175

1

The Wooing of Grain and Clay

Our education system should re-align itself at the earliest to meet the needs of the present day challenges and be fully geared to participate in societal transformation through innovation, which is the key to competitiveness.[1]

Do we all have the ability to excel in life or is it reserved for only a few? Is it the flash of insight or solution to a nagging problem that differentiates between the mundane and brilliant, ordinary and successful? Is it an earthly norm or is it of the divine? Questions of a similar nature were hovering in my mind when I went to Switzerland in October 2004 and sat on the chair of Albert Einstein (1879-1955) in his study. Perhaps one might not have imagined that Einstein would change the understanding of mankind when he emerged from the patent office in 1905, carrying his three brilliant manuscripts.[2] Einstein was blessed with success to become one of the most outstanding scientists of the 20th century. But what about many other innovative artists and scientists whose ideas were rejected by their contemporaries—Nicolaus Copernicus (1473-1543), Galileo Galilei (1564-1642), and even Charles Darwin (1809-1882). To say that Isaac Newton (1643-1727) discovered gravity or that Thomas Alva Edison (1847-1931) invented the electric bulb is a convenient simplification. What would have happened to the extraordinary albeit untutored brilliance of Srinivas Ramanujan (1887-1920) if it had not been articulated by British mathematician C.H. Hardy (1877-1947)? Would not Newton's or Edison's discoveries be inconceivable without the prior knowledge, the intellectual and social network that stimulated their thinking, or an emergent future that needed their innovations? There is definitely originality in the individual, but there is something more to captivate it.

This book is about this theme and the sub-routines around it. It is about the guidance that is received from the Universe. When the conditions are just right, solutions emerge in a guided way. The idea that continents drift around the planet on vast plates was considered preposterous for decades, but now we predict earthquakes based on this knowledge.[3] Similarly, it was not until William Harvey (1578-1657) that mankind knew about closed-loop circulation of blood inside the body with the heart as a pump.

Based on my experience, I can say that there is almost always a period of quiescence, a long spell of serenity and calm; a trial testing your patience, intent and perseverance. Then, suddenly, the full-blown solution emerges, which was otherwise impossible to perceive as if from a divine source. In Islamic parlance, the term used for this guidance is *ma'refat.* In Eastern religions, it is called *bodhi* (enlightenment). Western civilisation calls it *intuition.*

My exchanges with my contemporaries who know about it first hand led me to reflect upon some great thoughts written in different ages. I visualise life as a learning process. There is a gradual process of acquiring knowledge and education which prepares an individual for life. Education encompasses teaching and learning specific skills, and also something less tangible but more profound: imparting good judgement *(viveka)* and wisdom. Above all, education is a vehicle of culture from generation to generation. A good education system must, therefore, investigate the structure, materials and the condition of cultural property *(sanskriti)*. Moreover, the apparatus of education also carries upon it the responsibility of identifying the extent and cause of alteration and deterioration of culture. There have been phases of great turmoil and upheaval in history marked by immense misery and sufferings. There is no guarantee that there will be no further conflicts. Do we have a safeguard? When there is a rift, liberal education provides perspective and enables us to see life as a self-healing system.[4] Where do we begin?

To me, teaching people how to work out the truth for themselves—who they are and how they are connected to their surroundings—is a fairly good start for education. However, I realise that this is an unfashionable view in our times of 'no absolute truths'—where all knowledge is incomplete, evolving and relative to some cultural construction. The ignorance of those who seek realities in words and other constructs of mind and erred wildly therein is indeed beyond belief. Through this book, I want to put a cautionary word to those who are governing education.

Italian philosopher Giovanni Battista Vico (1668-1744) distinguished three 'instincts' which, he said shaped history, and three 'punishments' that shaped civilisation. The three instincts were (1) a belief in providence, (2) the recognition of parenthood, and (3) the instinct to bury the dead, which gave mankind institutions of religion, family and sepulchre. The three punishments were (1) shame, (2) curiosity, and the (3) need to work.[5]

The wonderful things that are taught in our schools are indeed the work of many generations, produced by enthusiastic effort and infinite labour in every country of the world. All this is put into the hands of young students as their inheritance in order that they may receive it, honour it and add to it in good faith that one day, they can faithfully pass it on to their children. We mortals do achieve immortality in the permanent things which we create in common. If we always keep that in mind, we will find meaning in life and work and acquire the right attitude towards other nations and ages.

My spiritual roots come from the multi-religious environment of Rameswaram Island. I grew up amidst the sound of prayer calls from the mosque, church bells and the temple music, all three interfused and yet distinct. I lived in an island where everything – the sea, the moon, the seagulls, the sand, the shells, the pilgrims, the porters, the coconut trees – was interconnected.

The concept of *Tawhid* is the central tenet of Islam. Each one of us is guided by conditions in the environment. Nothing exists in isolation, be it a celestial body, a particle of sand, a bird or a human being. There is a purpose behind every entity. The concept of *Tawhid* explains an idea that innovation arises not from the mind of a single individual but from the synergy of multiple sources.[6] A genuinely creative accomplishment is almost never the result of a sudden insight, a flash of lightning in the dark, but comes after years of hard work.

This guidance is, indeed, a central source of meaning in our lives for several reasons. Whatever I am, the language I speak, the values I hold dear, my expression, my scientific understanding, the technology with which I laboured, is the result of a long process of creation. So many individual ingenuities were fused to create whatever I thought or did.

All my achievements for which I was recognised and

rewarded were, indeed, transmitted to me through learning. I wonder what I could have learnt without inputs that were always available to me. I also felt that when I was deeply involved with my work, I was living more fully than during the periods of inaction and rest. My work provided me with a profound sense of being part of an entity greater than myself. But can I then sum up my life as my work?

There were several turning points in my life. These turning points telescope years of hardship, doubt and confusion. It is not that my hard work was always rewarded; the toil was redeemed by success. There are high points for which I am known—SLV-3, Agni, Vision 2020, Pokharan tests and perhaps Presidency—but hidden behind them was a great learning history, the sloppy, trial-and-error solutions to small problems. And there were so many failures. It is impossible to understand what happens in the mind of an individual when solutions finally arrive. I can only feel grateful to my teachers who gave me an assured ground on which I stood firm to face all that had come my way.

In September 2005, I visited Enchey Monastery in Sikkim. Later, I interacted with the students at Sir Tashi Namgyal Senior Secondary School in Gangtok. I discussed the education with the abbot of the monastery, who recited Kalama Sutra.

> *I will teach you the truth and the path leading to the truth. It is proper for you to doubt ... do not go by report ... do not go by tradition ... do not go by hearsay. Human life is just like a mountain river, flowing far and swift, taking everything along with it; there is no moment, no instant, no second when it stops flowing, but it goes on flowing and continuing. Rely not on theory, but on experience.*[7]

In September 2006, I went to Beschi College in Dindigul to meet Rev. Fr. Ladislaus Chinnathurai, who taught me Physics in 1950's at St. Joseph's College, Trichchirapalli. Rev. Father told me that plants are shaped by cultivation and men by education. We are born weak; we need strength; we are born totally unprovided; we need aid; we are born with plain awareness; we need judgement and discern. As we grow, education provides for all our needs.

In Greek mythology, the human experience is, indeed, guided by entities. There are three Muses: *Aoide* (voice or song), *Melete* (practice or occasion) and *Mneme* (memory). The Greeks believed that Muses were the key to good life and brought about both prosperity and friendship.

> *O Muse!*
> *The causes and the crimes relate;*
> *What goddess was provoked, and whence her hate.*[8]

Imam Abu Hamid al-Gazzali (1058-1111) wrote that it is human effort that decides the value of one's life:

> *Men are divided into (1) those who take notice by themselves and understand (2) those who do not understand except through warning and instruction, and (3) those who benefit from neither, is like the division of the bosom of the earth into three parts: (1) where water collects and increases till it bursts out by itself into springs of living water, (2) where water collects but cannot be reached without digging, and (3) arid parts where not even digging will avail.*[9]

Therefore, a combination of talent and effort determines the quality of human life. The origin of talent and the source that inspire effort remains a matter of mystery. Different cultures offer different rationales.

It was during Renaissance in Europe that the term 'creativity' came to be known to describe a sense of human independence of thought and freedom of expression. Spanish writer Baltasar Gracian (1601-1658) described art as the completion of nature. By the 18th century, the concept of creativity was linked with the concept of imagination, the power and process of producing mental images and ideas. In the 19th century, art alone was regarded as creative. At the turn of the 20th century, creativity was generally taken as the transference to the sciences of concepts proper to art.

Hungarian-born British Arthur Koestler (1905-1983) described three types of creative individuals—the Artist, the Sage, and the Jester. He held that all three elements were necessary in a creative process. Koestler introduced the concept of analogical thinking; he termed it as *bisociation.* According to this concept, creation of a new mental form is the result of the intersection of two quite different frames of reference in the mind.[10]

In the Geneplore model of creativity[11], developed a decade ago, it is held that creativity is a generative process. There is an individual construct of mental representations called pre-inventive structures, and there is an exploratory phase where these structures are used to come up with hitherto non-existent creative ideas.

In the contemporary computer age, creativity is seen as a process of iteration, an evolutionary computation. Generally, most creative techniques use associations between the goals and the problem. The current state, which may be an imperfect solution to the problem, is used to pick up stimulants randomly, leading to creative solutions. Three of the best-known techniques in vogue are brainstorming, lateral thinking and inventive problem-solving. The shift from a mystical origin of creativity to an iterative group activity is both evolutionary and revolutionary.

What is there which is revolutionary in the established evolutionary trajectory of 5000 years? What is it that stands unique in the present age? I believe it is expounding of knowledge. Knowledge is the most powerful force at the moment that is leading human societies to newer forms of existence. The Internet-driven society presents great opportunities: it can mean newer employment possibilities, more fulfilling jobs, new tools for education and training, easier access to public services, increased inclusion of so far marginalised people or regions. It is revolutionary, but what is this revolution doing?

For the first time in Indian history, four generations of people now work together. Each generation needs to know about it and others in order to make age diversity strong instead of weak. I will start with my generation, born before independence. Let me call it the *Quiet Generation*. We, as children, were taught to rely on tried, true and tested ways of doing things. After decades of working under command-and-control management, we believed in dedication, commitment, loyalty and a hard day's work. We perceived the changes as more radical than any other generation and are often sceptical about the changes that are imminent. Having amassed invaluable knowledge, we have considerable experience and wisdom to offer to the younger generations. If you are a member of the *Quiet Generation*, you probably recognise that cutting-edge ideas and new technologies will help you stay on top of your profession.

Avoid being stereotyped as the older person who stubbornly refuses to change, but don't be afraid to tap into your experience to discern what is ephemeral and what is essential. If you are not confident of your technological skills, identify techno-savvy younger colleagues and partner with them for two-way coaching. You need their technological expertise and they need your skills in areas such as listening, conflict resolution and problem-solving.

Making up about one-third of today's workforce are the people born in independent India. I call them *Idealists.* These people paid their dues and climbed the ladder under the old rungs of establishment and now find themselves operating under the new. They are learning from younger generation that insist on work/life balance and being loyal to their families is not being self-centred; rather it is a healthy attitude of responsibility to themselves and others. After watching their juniors get hiring-bonuses and choice schedules, many of them are adopting the free-agent mindset and asking for the respect and recognition they deserve in return for their significant contributions.

If you are an *Idealist,* you may still have many productive work years ahead of you. Continue to scout out the training, support and resource you need to stay on top of your profession. Capitalise on the contributions you have made and learn how to negotiate the best deals for yourself. Join the *Quiets* in coaching and mentoring their younger generations. If you are in a position of authority, the key to gaining credibility, trust and respect with younger colleagues is to find and develop the leadership talent in your team.

People born after the Green Revolution of the late 1960s were the first generation to recognise from day one that the dream of job security was a myth. Their free-agent attitude was outlandish to loyal, hardworking *Quiets* and *Idealists,* who considered them arrogant, disloyal slackers unwilling to pay their dues. I call them *Pushers.* During the past decade, however, *Pushers* brought about the IT revolution and indeed proved themselves to be valuable, creative contributors whose drive to get things done smarter, faster, safer and better has prompted workplace changes that every generation can embrace.

Pushers demand more transparency. Under their pressure, pay-for-performance became a reality in many organisations. If you are a *Pusher,* you may soon find yourself moving into positions of supervisory responsibility and leadership. Your mandate is to manage others the way you always wanted to be managed. Learn, practise and master the skills of the coaching-style manager.

If management is not your goal, you still want to learn marketable skills that will make you more valuable throughout your career. Prove your worth by making significant contributions every day and get involved in ongoing learning opportunities as a reward. Also, make sure your manager knows you are open to tackling newer areas of responsibility. Some older managers don't understand that giving you more responsibility isn't a punishment—as it was for their generation—but an opportunity to prove your worth and continue learning.

About a quarter of today's workforce is *Global* in their attitudes. Mostly, the children of *Idealists* believe education is the key to their success; technology is a transparent medium; diversity is given and social responsibility is a business imperative. They are *Global* because certain opportunities come from outside their country, particularly the United States and also West Asia. This generation thrives on the adrenalin rush of new challenges and new opportunities. *Globals* are highly paid due to their potential to become the highest-producing workforce in Indian history. Managers need to appreciate *Globals'* capabilities and help them test their limits.

If you are a *Global,* look for mentors and coaches to serve as experienced guides who can help you define what will make you succeed in your career and in your life. Learn how to ask searching questions and listen patiently to those who have walked the path you want to tread and who have the competencies you would like to master. Look for lessons that affect your life; take them to heart and make people proud for having coached and guided you.

All generations must understand that in the 21st century workplace, no needs or expectations of the generation have a monopoly. Everyone must be flexible, techno-savvy and knowledgeable, focusing on getting great work done every day. Consider yourself a free agent, responsible for your life, career, family and contributions. The workplace, in return, should recognise and reward your contributions accordingly.

So this is the soil, the ground for everyone. Educational levels are rising rapidly; rates of technological innovation and application are accelerating; cheaper and faster communication is dissolving physical and social barriers, both within the country and internationally; information is being made available in greater quantity and quality than ever before; and globalisation is opening up new markets. All seeds must find a place to germinate in this milieu.

The clay is whitening in the windy light
Where the sparrows are bathing.
Tomorrow surely
The seed will go under the harrow
Nothing must hinder
The wooing of grain and clay.[12]

The contemporary Republic of India is a young developing nation, but our people have a rich and illustrious history as one of the longest living civilisations in the world. Chinese author Lin Yutang (1895-1976) wrote:

The contact with poets, forest saints and the best wits of the land, the glimpse into the first awakening of India's mind as it searched, at times childishly and naively, at times with a deep intuition, but at all times earnestly and passionately, for the spiritual truths and the meaning of existence — this experience must be highly stimulating to anyone, particularly because the Indian culture is so different and, therefore, has so much to offer.[13]

To say that in 1947, India began to construct a modern nation would only be serving the ego of political leadership. In reality, Indians began the process of rediscovering their rich cultural and spiritual values that had formed the foundation of India in the past. Mahatma Gandhi (1869-1948) was a living representation of that process. Political leaders who eventually took charge of the independent nations of India and Pakistan emerged from that process.

Sixty years of walking on the post-independence road, the Indian nation faces a fork ahead: paraphrasing Scottish-American pastoral poet Robert Frost (1874-1963), two roads diverge ahead: (1) move on a business-as-usual basis or (2) evolve best case scenarios; clearly specifying the policies needed to move from one scenario to the other and also the hazards and risks of sticking only to the business-as-usual path.

The rapid development of the Information and Communication Technology (ICT) has brought about deep changes in our way of working and living, particularly in the urban areas. As the widespread diffusion of ICT is accompanied by organisational, commercial, social and legal innovations, low-cost information and ICT are in general use. The most valuable asset of India is its human and social capital and the key factors to develop these assets are knowledge and creativity.[14] More than half of India lives in villages and immense social and human capital is locked-up there for want of physical and knowledge connectivity. I dream of rural connectivity.

Best scenario forming cannot be an economic exercise.[15] It must include aspirations of all walks of life of common people. Developing India cannot be an anxious attempt to imitate and catch up with the developed countries. An intelligent emulation must draw upon the discoveries and experiences of others to address universal needs common to all human beings and all societies. India with its rich cultural heritage and thousands of years of history of civilisation need not aspire to become like one country or the other. For India, realising the vision for 2020 is not an end in itself, but rather an essential condition for allowing the seed-spirit of this country to germinate in the Globalised clay of the 21st century world and flourish.

Reality puts boundaries on what is needed and what is useful. Nothing will happen with the ideas unless there are selection mechanisms in place. You get many new ideas, but no one knows which are good or bad, and you have far more ideas than you can ever implement. Ultimately, you are just alienating several people whose new ideas are not feasible, whose aspirations are not finding place in your box. Roman Emperor Marcus Aurelius (121-180) wrote:

All things are woven together and the common bond is sacred, and scarcely one thing is foreign to another, for they have been arranged together in their places and together make the same ordered Universe. For there is one Universe out of all, one God through all, one substance and one law, one common Reason of all intelligent creatures and one Truth. Frequently consider the connection of all things in the Universe. We should not say I am an Athenian or I am a Roman but I am a citizen of the Universe.[16]

The proof of a mind's vigour depends on its ability to work on the material it meets with. A democracy can't draw strength out of the backwardness of its people. In fact, education is even more essential in a democratic society. Civilisations are like a web; they are not statues but great creations of individual genius.

A large number of youth approached me on the issue of reservations in education and employment based on socio-economic realities. We, as a society, need to distinguish between ideas that serve personal satisfaction and fulfilment, and what implies wider societal acceptance.

The Indian youth, indeed, faces the twin problems of the provision of quality education and unemployment to a large number of people. There are high aspirations to enter into institutions of higher learning such as engineering, medical and specialised sciences. This entry is through a vicious competition. A large number of students coming from backward communities find themselves handicapped and complain of an uneven level field. There is an urgent need to open up more student vacancies in centres of higher education as a mission. It requires a big investment but it can be achieved through public-private partnerships.

I am working on a system of global human resource cadre. In the 21st century, India needs a large number of talented youth with higher education for the task of knowledge acquisition, knowledge imparting, knowledge creation and knowledge sharing. The universities should set up special cadres to meet future demands, from both within and outside the country, of skilled and qualified young men and women.

The metaphor of interaction between clay—the milieu of learning opportunities—and grain—the potential of human mind—captures the essence of the contemporary world. If we can unveil the spectacle of the genius of a nation, we should find links between the common and uncommon in every walk of life. Algerian-French writer Albert Camus (1913-1960) wrote so aptly, "*Don't walk in front of me; I may not follow. Don't walk behind me; I may not lead. Just walk beside me and be my friend.*"[17]

□

2

In the Childhood Garden

When life is seen as a journey, it cannot be a race. A journey essentially savours each step of the way. What does this mean? As one progresses from the given starting conditions, each step involves growth. However, at each step, there is also competition. The competitors come from different starting conditions, mostly advantageous, and also the field is frequently uneven. Sages cautioned against undermining your worth by comparing yourself with others. Although comparing and contrasting is a valuable human skill yet problems arise when a comparing mind is the only mode of perception we access. If you

A nation is great, not because a few people are great, but because everyone in the nation is great. I visualise a Web of Life holding together and feeding the grass-root of our Society with nutrients of our technological strength and industrial prosperity.[18]

perceive yourself better than others, pride sets in. If you perceive yourself inferior to others, you lose self-esteem. When you do something, you should burn yourself completely, like a good bonfire, leaving no trace of yourself.[19] Each one of us is special because we are different. Whatever Nature creates is useful. Nature does not discriminate. Outside the realm of human perception, the concept of better or worse is meaningless.

Wise men cautioned against imitation. Amongst the three methods of learning wisdom: (1) reflection, (2) experience, and (3) imitation, Confucius (551-479 BC) termed reflection the noblest; experience the most bitter and imitation the easiest. Do not set your goals by what other people consider important. Ralph Waldo Emerson (1803-1882) said, *"There comes a time in every man's education when he arrives at the conviction that envy is ignorance, that imitation is suicide, that he must take himself for better, or for worse as his portion."* Only you know what is best for you. Do not take for granted the things closest to your heart. Cling to them as you will to your life, for without them, life is meaningless.

Scriptures celebrated perseverance. *"I returned, and saw under the sun, that the race is not to the swift, nor the battle to the strong, neither yet bread to the wise, nor yet riches to men of understanding, nor yet favour to men of skill; but time and chance happen to them all."*[20] The road to success is dotted with many tempting parking places. Do not give up when you still have something to give. Nothing is really over till the moment you stop trying. It is a fragile thread that binds us to one another.

The learned demand courage. Do not be afraid to encounter risks. It is by taking chances that we learn how to be brave. Mark Twain (1835-1910) wrote, *"Courage is resistance to fear, mastery of fear—not absence of fear."* American social activist, Clare Booth Luce (1903-1987), described *courage as the ladder on which all the other virtues mount.* First female pilot Amelia Earhart (1897-1937) defined that *courage as the price that life exacts for granting peace.*

I remember a scene. I flew a Sukhoi-30 MKI fighter plane on June 8, 2006, from Lohegaon airport near Pune. I was in the cockpit for 40 minutes with Wing Commander Ajay Rathore as my co-pilot. When we disembarked, someone asked me "You are a courageous President. In spite of being 75, did you not fear?" I said, "I did not have time to fear as I was continuously busy with the control of the instruments of the aircraft." Courage is doing nothing but an activity that you like. This is what good education teaches.

Above all, we must never dismiss our dreams. To be without dreams is to be without hope. To be without hope is to be without purpose. Irish playwright and essayist, Nobel Laureate, George Bernard Shaw (1856-1950), wrote, *"You see things; and you say, 'Why?' But I dream things that never were; and I say, 'Why not?'"* Another Irish Nobel Prize-winning poet, William Butler Yeats (1865-1939), wrote, *"In dreams begins responsibility."*[21] I believe that dreams transform into thoughts and thoughts transform into actions.

I find it very rewarding when I reflect on what happens to exceptional individuals from early childhood to old age. It is my belief that every life carries possibilities with it. The difference comes from the way life is encountered. I enjoy reading the biographies of successful people, for the story of each life teaches me newer lessons. After examining in the first chapter, a highly diverse socio-economic milieu where opportunities and resources are competed fervently for, if not fiercely, this chapter will focus on working lives.

In fact, the hardest teaching is received and the toughest examinations are faced not in schools but, in the later years, out of schools. During the student-life, lessons are given and then exams are taken. In working-life, exams are first faced and lessons are then learnt. By observing successful people, one can, indeed, envisage ways of breaking out from the routine, from the constraints of genetic and social conditioning, to a fuller existence.

Does an individual resolution to shape life to suit one's own goal instead of letting external force rule one's destiny? I read sometime back the example of a bumblebee. The laws of aerodynamics as given in the textbooks prove that the bumblebee should be incapable of flight, as it does not have the capacity, in terms of wing size or beat per second, to achieve flight with the degree of wing loading necessary. Not being aware that the scientists have proved that it cannot fly, the bumblebee succeeds. One shouldn't be surprised that the results of the calculations don't square with reality.

It took me a while to understand the bumblebee. The calculations which purported to show that bumblebees cannot fly, indeed, are based upon a simplified linear treatment of oscillating aerofoil. The method assumes small amplitude oscillations without flow separation. This ignores the effect of dynamic stall, an airflow separation inducing a large vortex above the wing, which briefly produces several times the lift of the aerofoil in regular flight. More sophisticated aerodynamic analysis validates the bumblebee's flight because its wings encounter dynamic stall in every oscillation cycle.

Indeed, it can be concluded that the most obvious achievement of human beings is that they crafted their own lives. And how they achieve it is something worth knowing, because it can be applied to our own lives, whether or not we are going to make a creative contribution.

This chapter presents an exploration of human potential that can be expanded just as naturally as a seed germinates to become a plant. There is increasing dialogue among religion, spirituality and science. Besides excellence in science, technology and arts, there is tremendous human potential for altruism, empathy and compassion waiting to manifest.[22]

There is nothing in the entire universe that exists without a purpose.[23] Purpose is central to a human life. The purpose of man's existence is not eating and sensual enjoyment. The holy Quran cautioned that fire will be the abode of those who enjoy themselves and eat as cattle eat.[24]

The mind's sensitivity to the meaning of life is, however, impaired by fixed notions or perspectives on what it means to be a human being. There is an infinite continuity of meaning that can be comprehended only by seeing again, for ourselves.

Unaware and almost every day, we read stories; we tell stories. Why is there a widespread tendency to weave around stories from the bits and pieces of life events? There is hardly any good story that can be called pure truth. The same seems to be true for the records of lives of great people. They reflect our psychological need more than reality. If someone becomes outstanding, we want to believe that unmistakable signs of greatness were there early on, for all to see. Whether it is the Buddha, Jesus, Edison, Einstein, Ramanujan or M.S. Subbulakshmi, we are so eager to believe that genius must have revealed itself in the earliest years of life.

As an example, a story Einstein liked to tell about his childhood was of a 'wonder' he saw when he was four or five years old: a magnetic compass. The invariable northward swing of the needle, guided by an invisible force, profoundly impressed the child. The compass convinced him that there had to be "something behind things, something deeply hidden." Even as a small boy, Einstein was self-sufficient and thoughtful.

Basing one's judgement on a child's early talents, it is impossible to tell, in most cases, whether he or she will be creative or not. Few children do show signs of extraordinary precocity early on in some domain or the other: Subbulakshmi was an accomplished singer at an early age; Ramanujan's passion with numbers was evident even when he was a boy. Many great scientists skipped grades in school and astonished their elders with the nimbleness of their minds. But there were many other children whose early promise fizzled out without leaving any trace in the history books. The Indian Government conducts Science Talent Search in schools every year. Only a few of them go on to become scientists.

Children can show tremendous talent, but they cannot be inventive because invention involves changing a way of doing things, or a way of thinking. For this, the first step is master the old ways of doing or thinking. Subbulakshmi in her teens might have been as accomplished as many singers alive, but she could not have changed the way people listened to music until her way of singing was taken seriously. For this to happen, she had to spend, at least, a decade mastering a new style of rendering devotional music. Only then, she was able to produce a number of convincing performances.

In September 2003, I went to Alfred High School,

now known as Mahatma Gandhi High School, Rajkot. There I saw M.K. Gandhi's report card displayed with his other articles. There was nothing spectacular in the report card. In fact, the man who eventually changed the course of Indian history scored just 38 out of 100 in History in Class VIII exam.

What if the real childhood accomplishments of great individuals are no different from those of many others who never attain any distinction? The mind will do its best to weave appealing stories to compensate. What is the mechanism that generates such stories? Have we all not added imaginative content in our past to make our own lives, or those of young children in families, more interesting and more sensible?

When I visit schools, children ask me about my achievement during my childhood. My childhood was, in reality, not very descriptive. It was just like any other childhood of an islander boy. But children insist on a story. The most imaginative I could be without altering the truth is to relate my career in aeronautical engineering to my fifth standard teacher Siva Subramanian Iyer who took me to the seashore to explain how birds fly.

It is not because I am consciously trying to overemphasise this little event. It is because as one tells a tale over and over, the tendency is to highlight what in hindsight we feel are the important parts. Also, there is an unconscious attempt to eliminate details that contradict the point of the story. Our sense of inner consistency demands it and the audience will also appreciate the story more. With each explanation, my teacher's visits to the seashore along with the students becomes more remarkable. Perhaps, this is the process by which myths are created. There is always a story presenting the reality in an attractive form. Thus the apple that fell on Newton became more famous than the theory of gravitation and Archimedes' cries of 'Eureka!' was accepted in all languages of the world. It is for the story that as a child, Benjamin Franklin (1706-1790) tied a key bunch to a kite string, flew it in a thunderstorm and watched the lightning strike it. As another legend goes, young James Watt (1736-1819) watched how the lid was lifted off the kettle under the force of steam.

I will upset many if I say that whether a great child will be a great individual, is a big question. At best, we can ask what great individuals were like when they were children, or what sorts of events shaped the early lives of those who later accomplished something extraordinary.

When we look at what is known about the childhood of eminent people, it is difficult to find any consistent pattern. Young Einstein was no prodigy. Even a mature adult Indira Gandhi (1917-1984) was undermined before she actually took over as India's most commanding Prime Minister. Sarat Chandra Chattopadhyay (1876-1938), Maqbool Fida Hussain (b. 1915) and Amartya Sen (b. 1933) did not impress their elders as future geniuses. Unlike Ravi Shankar (b. 1920) who displayed unusual gift in music before his teens, A.R. (Allah Rakha) Rahman (b. 1966) blossomed only in his twenties. The early years provide at best only glimpses of extraordinary ability in the domain they eventually turned to.

If being a prodigy is not a requirement for later achievement, then what is it? I believe, in most cases, it is the parents and primary school teachers who are responsible for stimulating and directing the child's interest. Later, a mentor steps in. What do they exactly contribute? Let me share my personal experiences.

Strong parental influence is necessary for those children who are born into a poor or socially marginal set-up. Lacking other advantages, such as good schools and access to mentors, it is almost impossible to succeed without parental support and guidance. My father's stern ways of monitoring my education as well as how I spent my leisure time were mainly responsible for my strong personal regulation and self-confidence. The sense of self-respect and discipline I absorbed at home stood me in good stead later on. American teacher, Abraham Joshua Heschel (1907-1972), so aptly wrote, *"Self-respect is the fruit of discipline; the sense of dignity grows with the ability to say 'no' to oneself."*

It is very hard for me to describe what my parents were in intellectual terms. But one of the things, which I greatly appreciate, was that they were very generous. They never denied us help. And they were more than ever generous to me because I showed an aptitude for education. Later, my sister, Zohra, would also 'act' mother and lend me a helping hand so that I might opt for higher education by selling her jewellery for paying my fee.

My teacher, Iyadurai Solomon, was an ideal teacher for an eager young mind who was uncertain of the possibilities and alternatives that lay before him. He made us feel very comfortable in class with his warm and open-minded attitude. He used to say that a good student could learn more from a teacher than a poor student from even a skilled teacher. I have seen him giving free tuitions to many students who were not doing well in the class. Under his direction, I learnt that one could exercise enormous influence over the events of one's own life by making the right choices. He used to say, *"To succeed in life and achieve results, you must understand and master three mighty forces-desire, belief and expectation."* Iyadurai Solomon, later, became a Rev. Father.

Possibly, the most important contribution of parents and early teachers is in shaping character. Perhaps, the most important value parents can teach their children is honesty.

In work situations, the mentor takes up the place of parents. I had been extremely fortunate to have Brahm Prakash (1912-1984) who guided me. He kindly mended my ruthless and antagonistic ways of working. I believe that the responsibility of an authentic mentor is not only to be honest to himself but also to make sure of the honesty of his/her pupil. My connotation of 'honesty' here means authenticity in one's work. How can we be authentic?

You must criticise yourself; you must consider everything that may contradict what you think, and you must never conceal an error. The whole atmosphere should nurture this spirit. Later, when you are head of a lab or an institute, you must make a great effort to help those who are honest and not merely career-oriented. This is the most important task that a leader has. It is absolutely fundamental. I want to place the origin of these qualities in my own working to the mentoring of Brahm Prakash.

Our efforts will kindle their seeking mind then at last
We can give them the act - so sublime!
Be patient O my dear!
Give not into fear.
Give not in to concern, for what is so near.[25]

Who amongst us does not want to be successful in whatever is done? Each one of us enjoys the respect that goes with success and the sense of satisfaction that accompanies accomplishment. It is my firm belief that the foundation of a successful life rests on the triad of parents, teachers and mentors. What can you get of life, if you can't respect your parents, teachers and mentors? Of course, respect does not mean blind obedience. Free and honest thinking has no place for contradiction. However, contradiction should not debase into disrespectful arrogance.

I believe childhood is an indivisible part of one's

destiny. I attach enormous importance to my early memories. When I look back, it is inevitable that what we see now is coloured by what happened in the years in between. A person, who is relatively happy and content in the present, may remember more sunshine than there actually was. Similarly, someone wounded by life may project more misery into the past. I feel, most of the adults who feel positively about themselves describe their childhood in most favourable terms. Though it remains unclear which is the cause and which is the effect.

Even if the family and school were not a source of inspiration, when a child grows into teenage and enters college, there is always a teacher who arrives to awaken, sustain, or direct his or her interest. I am yet to find a person who cannot gratefully remember, at least, one teacher in college. My teachers at St. Joseph's College loaned their books to me and gave me tutorials and special tests to shape my abilities. How do we describe a good teacher?

In Buddhism, the teacher occupies the centre stage. The teacher must teach with the thought, "I will speak step-by-step." The teacher must teach with the thought, "I will speak explaining the sequence of cause and effect." The teacher must teach with the thought, "I will speak out of compassion." The teacher must teach with the thought, "I will speak not for the purpose of material reward." The teacher must teach with the thought, "I will speak without disparaging myself or others."[26]

Imam al-Gazzali regards the first duty of a teacher to accept the child unconditionally as his own. He quotes the saying of the Prophet of Islam: "I am to you like a father who desires to save his child from the fires of hell, which is more important than any of the efforts of parents to save their children from the fires of the earth."[27]

We can see that a teacher's concern is not only to achieve immediate and short-term success, such as good examination results, but to inculcate values which are formative, more permanent and will help his student to excel in this and the after-life. Imam al-Gazzali explains that education is a journey to *Allah*.

Another important duty is that the teacher should adapt the teaching to the child's level of intelligence and needs. Let me appeal to our teachers—do not neglect this basic duty and leave the innocent little children to grope helplessly in the dark as they struggle to understand the work which is above their present level of understanding.

This duty further implies that the teacher must know his children intimately and understand their problems so that he may help them overcome or cope with these problems.

Closely related to this duty is the teacher's duty to teach in such a manner that befits his dignity, authority and honour that the parents and children bestow on him. Let us remember that often it is not what we teach our children that will influence them, but how we teach it. Be patient when you wait for the slowest child to arrive at an answer. Show humility when you say to a child, "I don't know the answer; let us look it up!" It is the encouragement that you offer the slower child and the generous praise when he can master even a small part of the work! Are not we, as parents and teachers, the mirrors to our children? The dedicated teacher, according to Imam al-Gazzali, is like the wick of a lamp which burns itself out in giving light to others.[26] Dr. S. Radhakrishnan (1888-1975) saw a teacher as a guide, "In our life, the direction and goal of which is lost in the infinite."

On Teacher's Day 2006, I administered a 10-point oath during the presentation of National awards to meritorious teachers. The oath goes like this: (1) First and foremost, I will love teaching. Teaching will be my soul. Teaching will be my life's mission; (2) I realise by being a teacher, I am making an important contribution to the efforts of national development; (3) I realise that I am responsible not only for shaping students but also for igniting youth who are the most powerful resource under the earth, on the earth and above the earth; (4) I will consider myself to be a great teacher only when I am capable of elevating the average student to the high performance and when no student is left out as a non-performer; (5) I will organise and conduct my life, in such a way that my life itself is a message for my students; (6) I will encourage my students to ask questions and to seek answers in order to develop the spirit of enquiry, and they blossom into creative enlightened citizens;

(7) I will treat all the students equally and will not support any differentiation on account of religion, community or language; (8) I will continuously build my own capacities in teaching so that I may impart quality education to my students; (9) I will constantly endeavour to fill my mind, with great thoughts and spread the nobility in thinking and action among my students; and (10) I will always celebrate the success of my students.

If so much is expected of the teacher in the educational situation, how much more is not expected of the student? The student's first duty is to develop noble qualities such as truthfulness, sincerity, piety and humility. This, Imam al-Gazzali calls "the adornment and beautification of the inner self." With a beautiful inner self, with a pure heart, with noble intentions, we approach our learning.

Like the teacher, a student must, at all times, be humble. As long as students are proud and arrogant, and as long as they are filled with self-glory, they will not hear or see anything else. Even the teacher's guidance will mean nothing to them. I read somewhere:

"Knowledge humbles the haughty youth,
As the flood washes away the hill."

Humility is the key to successful learning. Yes, but don't become so submissive to your teachers that you are too meek to ask questions in order to improve your understanding. Your teachers would expect you to question them, to participate actively and to contribute to the lessons. It is the right of every student to get up in the classroom and be heard. It is the students' right to contribute to the organisation of the college through student councils and other such bodies. It is their right to help decide what they need to know, a privilege that cannot be denied to them. Similarly, it is their duty to respect the authority and dignity of the teacher as extension of their parents.

Hazrat Inayat Khan[28] expressed it this way:

"Knowledge will surrender nothing to man
Unless man surrenders his all to it."

Talented teenagers have some special obstacles to surmount. Popularity is a big trap in teenage. None of the creative people I know recall being popular in their adolescence. Some of them told me that they, indeed, had a reasonably troubled time getting along with their friends. Marginality—the feeling of being on the outside, of being different, of observing with detachment the strange rituals of one's peers—appears a common theme. I was a marginal myself, marginal to the upper class, marginal to my school friends, and so on, but also marginal because of my views. At times, I was even insulted. Rumi's words inspired me:

If an ant seeks the rank of Solomon, don't smile contemptuously upon its quest. Everything you possess of skill, and wealth and handicraft, wasn't it first merely a thought and a quest? [29]

There are multiple threads of continuity from childhood to adulthood. In some cases, the continuity of interest from childhood to later life is direct; in others, it is strangely convoluted. For each creative person, whose life seems like a seamless unfolding from childhood into old age, or whose interests seem preordained even before birth, there is another whose later career seems to be the product of chance or of an interest that appears seemingly out of nowhere long after the early years have past.

What shapes creative lives? We, in India, are used to take life in a fatalistic fashion. But reflecting on the lives of creative individuals brings out a different set of possibilities. If the future is indeed determined by the past, we should be able to see clearer patterns which are, by and large, absent. There is a great variety of paths that led people to eminence. It seems to me that men and women are not shaped, once and for all, either by their genes or by the events of early life. Rather, as they moved along with time, being bombarded by external events, encountering good and bad people, good and bad breaks, they had to make do with whatever came to hand. Instead of being shaped by events, they shape events to suit their purposes.

So, it appears that a creative life is determined, but what determines it is not the genes, family, school, or even college. There is a will moving across time and a fierce determination to succeed. Of course, this still leaves the question—so where does this will and determination come from? Is it genetically programmed sensitivity, stimulating early experiences? Is not the teacher stepping into the Universe to offer guidance?

In India's great epic, the *Mahabharata*, as the battle is about to begin, Arjuna, himself an acclaimed warrior, wonders how he could kill his own blood relatives with whom he had grown up as a child. He puts the battle on hold and begins a conversation with Lord Krishna. *The Bhagavad-Gita* (The Song of God) begins here and ends with Lord Krishna convincing Arjuna that in the grand scheme of things, he is only a pawn. The best he could do is by doing his duty and not question God's will.

The law of universal causality represents the core of Indian spirituality. It connects man with the Cosmos and fixes the responsibility of every action performed. There is a concept of transmigration—to move from one body to another after death—indefinitely till the consequence of every misdeed is experienced. The eternal soul, moving from body to body, ascends or descends the ladder of a given hierarchy, conditioned on the nature of one's own work of life or life deeds. Even if we choose not to know precisely from where we are ascending or descending, what is important is to feel the urge when it arises. Recognise the guidance when it shows itself, follow it and put in our best efforts.

□

3

The Treble of Heaven's Harmony

Success and struggle are, indeed, synonymous to life. Austrian neurologist and the founder of the Psychoanalytic School of Psychology, Sigmund Freud (1856-1939), wrote, *"One day, in retrospect, the years of struggle will strike you as the most beautiful."* To progress in life, one must make a tremendous effort to fight all the stumbling blocks that come across one's way. It is like climbing a flight of stairs or walking up a hill, which takes all of one's energy and effort. A strenuous journey to the pinnacle: the exhilaration is unsurpassable. Emily Dickinson (1830-1886) captured this thought as:

Conscience is the light of the Soul that burns within the chambers of our psychological heart.[30]

Success is counted sweetest
By those who ne'er succeed.
To comprehend a nectar
Requires sorest need.[31]

I have always appreciated life. I hold it sacred. Just as in any traditional Indian joint family, my early tutelage to life and learning was not only from my parents but from the elders at home. Later, my teacher, Siva Subramanian Iyer, and my mentor, Brahm Prakash, continued to be my support. They all were very good people, with incredible hearts and spirits and an endless capacity to love and understand. They were completely selfless and generous. There was a strange confidence in the way they lived. Each one of them, in his or her own unique way, trusted that the path of life was leading his/her to his/her destiny. They trusted the Universe and believed that it governed all.

Trusting the universe means living with a faith that no matter how much pain you are in, or how out of control everything around you appears, all the happenings are for a reason. It is about believing in a higher purpose of life. I have seen many people moving through life, oblivious to the beauty that is profuse all around. William Wordsworth (1770-1850) wrote:

Earth has not anything to show more fair:
Dull would he be of soul who could pass by
A sight so touching in its majesty.[32]

Often situations in life appear insurmountable and the easiest thing to do is give up. I, too, have had my fair share of ups and downs but recollect only a few that were insurmountable.

In 1972, both Satish Dhawan and Brahm Prakash called me. Chairman Dhawan said, "I am going to give you a very important project. You will be the Project Director for the SLV-3.[33] You will be provided the required budget. The project will be completed in seven years. All manpower will be available to you from the organisation—from all the centres. We all will work together as a team. I will report to you." I was surprised that he selected me for this position amongst the many senior scientists.

I wondered, "How am I going to do it?" Then Satish Dhawan gave me a piece of advice that I always remembered. "Kalam," he said, "if one does not venture out, he stays in his shell. When we take up a mission or task, problems are bound to arise. You must become the master of the problem, defeat that problem and succeed."

Seven years later, in August 1979, it was the countdown for the satellite launch vehicle. We all were in Sriharikota. During the final stages, we turned to auto-pilot mode. The computers warned us not to launch. I consulted with the other experts. They said, "Don't worry; launch it." Functioning as Mission Director, I bypassed the computer and took over the manual launch. The vehicle failed and sank into the Bay of Bengal. The Press asked how I could put Rs. 20 crore (200 million) into the Bay of Bengal.

It was the advice of Satish Dhawan combined with the spiritual strength inculcated from my family that helped me emerge out of the failure. Instead of brooding over the mishap, we turned our energy to conduct a root cause analysis in a very objective manner. Then M.R. Kurup, the Chairman of the Failure Analysis Board, along with G. Madhavan Nair as member-secretary, meticulously interviewed more than 125 scientists and staff, and analysed over 200 data records.

Finally, we could locate the fault to the air-conditioning plant. During the period before the launch, dust had entered the valve system of the control power plant, resulting in its improper functioning. After this incident, we ensured that all our systems went through rigorous quality checks. Not only could we fix the technical problem but we were also able to keep the morale of the scientists high, so much so that it enabled me to go for the next launch within one year. We succeeded in that attempt.

Another problem arose in 1989. The 'Agni launch'[34] was scheduled for April 20. When we were at T-14 second, the computer signalled 'hold', indicating that one of the instruments was functioning erratically. By that time, the umbilical connector, giving power to the missile on the launch pad, was disconnected. The missile electronic system was operating on batteries inside the subsystems. We recharged them.

We got the missile on the launch pad on May 1. But again, during the automatic computer check-out period at T-10 second, a 'hold' command was signalled. One of the control components was malfunctioning. The launch had to be aborted again. There was confusion all around, not only in the public domain but also in my laboratory at Hyderabad.

I invited the entire community of Defence Research & Development Laboratory (DRDL) and Research Centre Imarat (RCI) working on the missile projects. There were 2000 people standing at the main gate of DRDL that had seemed more like a public rally. I still recollect myself saying, "Very rarely does a laboratory get an opportunity to develop a system like 'Agni'. A great opportunity came our way. Naturally, major opportunities are accompanied by equally major challenges. We will not give up and we will not allow the problem to defeat us. The country does not deserve anything less than success from us. Let us aim for success." I found myself telling, "I promise you, we will be back after successfully launching 'Agni' before the end of this month." Was it a *ma'refat*? It eventually happened on May 22.

I want to reassure young children that all the pain that they inevitably go through in life is to allow them to evolve into accomplished individuals; develop a deeper understanding of who they are and where they belong to. Life is less stressful when we trust that we are always being guided for our highest good.

William Tiller, promoter of the concept 'subtle energies', writes that the Universe has a plan for our development and 'tilts' the statistics so that events and opportunities may be caused to appear in our paths. It is, therefore, sensible to do what is immediately at one's hand; do it with all of one's might and do it joyfully. Then move on without lingering attachments, with the confidence that the unfolding prospects will lead to our greater growth. According to Tiller, it is all right to stumble because such events show us what we still have to learn.[35]

A youth comes out of college with dreams and goals. When I graduated as an aeronautical engineer, I had a dream of flying a fighter aircraft. I appeared for entry into the Air Force, but failed to get in and had experienced times of insecurity and uncertainty concerning my future, and my place in this world. However, something deep within me always brought me comfort in times of despair. I must share with my readers this concept of the 'inner sanctuary'.

I always felt that there was a vast inner space in the mind. I often dwelt in this inner space and visualised how I would like my life to be, the places that I wanted to visit, and the person I wished to be. I would imagine myself achieve all that I wanted. This place to me was more real than even the immediate world around. It was like a secret treasure chest within, the place that you hold dear to your heart; the place where you hold your innermost dreams and desires.[36] William Wordsworth (1770-1850) so beautifully described this feeling:

For oft, when on my couch I lie
In vacant or in pensive mood,
They flash upon that inward eye
Which is the bliss of solitude.[37]

How does one find this treasure chest? Where is the key? Will finding the key propel me in the direction of my dreams, and allow me to realise and achieve them as a matter of luck or chance? Nobel Prize winner in Literature, Polish poetess, Wislawa Szymborska (b. 1923), writes:

There is so much everything
That nothing is hidden quite nicely.[38]

When we say that something new has been found or a long-felt need has been accomplished, it is, indeed, the culmination of a process that started long ago, not withstanding our awareness. Almost every invention including the most celebrated ones eventually appears as a projection of one's thought and nature.

Most achievements are a part of long-term commitment to a domain of interest. Every child is endowed with a natural frequency that takes his/her attention to certain areas. A certain interest starts building up somewhere in childhood, proceeds through schools and continues during university, a research laboratory, an artist's studio, a writer's table, or a business corporation.

The possibilities are enormous; occupational paths vary a great deal depending on the domain in which a person is active. The career of a poet is very different from that of a nuclear-physicist or a cardiologist or the CEO of a financial firm. Moreover, the career lines of men and women can vary a great deal even within the same sub-field. It is important to understand the knowledge-process that spans years, decades and even lifetimes.

British philosopher, Leslie J. Walker (1877-1958), described knowledge as a state of mind. He said, "A person initially starts with ignorance. The first step demands some knowledge which the person, all things considered, ought to possess. A surgeon need not know how 'eccentric' a steam engine is, but he ought to know what a 'tourniquet' is. *In itself, ignorance is nothing.*"

Next to ignorance, comes doubt. Doubt is the negation of a state of consciousness. It is simply the absence of belief and again is nothing by itself. The first step out of doubt may be called suspicion, which is described as so faint an inclination to yield in one direction, which is not yet apparent. A good analogy is elastic strain before the plastic reformation occurs in a structural element. There is an assent to the presence of load; though the element has not given into the load.

An opinion is expressed when an assent is given to the suspicion, though as to a mere probability and only under restriction. When a thing is held as a probable opinion or as certain, it becomes belief. It must not be confused with knowledge.

Knowledge is a certainty founded upon insight and belief is a certainty founded upon feeling. Belief is the primary condition of knowledge but not knowledge by itself. To believe that the sky is blue is to think that the proposition, "The sky is blue", is true. Most knowledgeable people indeed operate on beliefs. An assurance is said to be either knowledge or a belief, depending upon which of the two predominates.[39]

There are broadly two types of work ethos. One is the classical type where the career lines are laid out and one just needs to move along that said path. The other is of creative individuals who need to rediscover their work profiles constantly.

Most of us join an organisation at the entry level, perform a prescribed role for a number of years and leave at a higher level. A worker may start as a toolmaker and leave as a foreman; a teacher may teach for thirty years and become a principal; a soldier may become a sergeant; a young lawyer may end up as a partner of the firm, and so forth. These rules are relatively fixed, and we fit into them. I joined Defence Research & Development Organisation (DRDO) as a Senior Scientific Assistant and retired 40 years later as its chief, of course, with a twenty-year sojourn at Indian Space Research Organisation (ISRO). I merely followed career lines that were laid out for me.

On the other hand, creative individuals usually are forced to invent on the job they will be doing all through their lives. It is the group of these individuals who take a different path and discover a new dimension of creative energy. One could not have been a psychoanalyst before Freud, an aeronautical engineer before the Wright brothers, an electrician before Edison. Before Jamshedji Tata (1839-1904), there was no steel-making in India, and there was no space research before Vikram Sarabhai (1919-1971). I personally know two men who excelled outside their 'spheres'. Verghese Kurien (b. 1921), mechanical engineer, created the milk co-operative movement in India working with farmers; and cardiologists B. Soma Raju (b. 1946) made a coronary stent with defence scientists. These individuals not only discovered new ways of thinking and of doing things but also became the first practitioners in the domains they discovered and made it possible for others to have jobs and careers in the new enterprises.

Pioneers must create a field that will nurture their ideas, as new ideas cannot survive for long without finding acceptance in the culture of the day. Kurien had to convince farmers about his ideas and Soma Raju had to attract engineers to his work, because careers can take place only within fields. If a person wants to have a career in a field that does not exist, he or she must invent it. And that is what people, who create new domains, do.

What happens to writers, musicians and artists? These are some of the oldest professions. So, it must be wrong to claim that a creative poet creates the role of a poet. There is a very real sense in which this is actually true. Each poet, musician, or artist, who leaves an impression, must find a way to write, compose, or paint like no one has done before. While the role of artists is an old one, the substance of what they do is unprecedented. Two examples, one from the sciences and one from the arts, that I came across, illustrate what is involved in creating creative careers.

We were working with high strength composite materials to make missile heat shield when orthopaedic surgeon, B.N. Prasad, approached me to develop Floor Reaction Orthosis, a prosthesis with which polio-affected children could walk more conveniently and comfortably. Father Felix started the first school for the mentally retarded at Changanacherry in Kottayam district in Kerala and developed new ways of coping with disability with a new kind of dance training.

Work alone remains after the death of any individual. The present generations know Ramakrishna Paramhans, Dayanand Saraswati and Aurobindo Ghosh when young children go to study in the schools founded by them, in the past. To mortals like us, immortality can become a reality only through the significant work we leave behind.

Immortality is, indeed, a genetically carried delusion. For some strange reason, no one wants to die. It is much easier to come to terms with one's mortality when one knows that parts of one will continue to live on after one's death in the form of his/her work of lasting value.

There is often a presumption that only one way out of two possible ways of living after death—physical in the form of children or mental in the form of books—is permissible. The Romans had a saying—*libri aut liberi* (books or children). It refers to how difficult it was to have it both ways. In fact, in many cultures, it has been the case that those who wrote the books—the monks in early Christendom, the Tibetan lamas, or Buddhist monks and Sufi's—were not supposed to have married life and children. I feel that I unconsciously followed this tradition.

The second most potent desire after immortality is to lead. Man is bestowed with a trait to preside over other creatures on the earth. This trait overdeveloped into a desire to lead fellow beings and govern their affairs. One can govern oneself, or one can govern the whole earth. In between, we may find leaders who operate primarily within families, communities, states and nations. Intertwined with such categories, and overlapping them, we find religious leaders, workplace leaders such as executives, officers, managers, team-leaders, supervisors and leaders of voluntary associations. Though there are many stories to make us believe that charisma and personality worked miracles, most leaders operate within a structure of supporters and executive agents who carry out and monitor the expressed or filtered-down will of the leader. This undercutting of the importance of leadership may serve as a reminder of the existence of the follower.

Leading and managing are two different ways of organising people. The manager uses a formal, rational method, while the leader uses passion and stirs emotions. A leader is someone whom people naturally follow by choice, whereas a manager must be obeyed. A manager may only have obtained his position of authority through time and loyalty given and not as a result of his leadership qualities. A leader may have no organisational skills, but his vision unites people.

Leaders are innately observant and sensitive people. They know their team and develop mutual confidence within it. Leaders stand out by being different. They question assumption and are suspicious of tradition. They seek the truth and make decisions based on facts.

In modern dynamic environments, formal bureaucratic organisations have become less common because of their inability to deal with rapidly changing circumstances. Most modern business organisations and some government departments indeed encourage what they see as *leadership skills* and reward identified potential leaders with promotions. To stress this point, we can examine the success story of Bill Gates. He founded Microsoft as the 21st century organisation, and runs it with a sense of vision 20 years ahead of his time. For a vision to succeed, it must be shared. Today, 76,000 workforce in 102 countries share Bill Gates' vision to create an annual revenue of over US$44 billion. How is it done?

An effective leader unites followers in a shared vision

that will improve an organisation and the society at large. Good leadership must deliver 'true' value. This can happen only through integrity and trust. Thus, transformational leadership is different from a transactional leadership which builds power by doing whatever that results in more followers.

The metaphor of an orchestra conductor can best describe the leadership process. An effective leader resembles an orchestra conductor in many ways. The leader gets a group of potentially diverse and talented people—many of whom have strong personalities—to work together towards a common goal. The efficiency of the orchestra just as in leadership will best be represented if the conductor can harness and blend all the gifts his or her players possess if the players accept the degree of creative expression they have. The conductor or leader must have a strong determining influence on the complete performance.

The scientific leadership theory[40] identifies six critical capabilities that are grouped under Leadership Capital and four capacities termed Leadership conditions. The six critical Leadership Capital capacities are: (1) vision, (2) values, (3) wisdom, (4) courage, (5) trust, and (6) expression. The four vital Leadership conditions necessary for these capacities to make a difference are: (1) a place where the leader can hold sway, (2) a period that calls for his or her leadership, (3) a position that conveys leadership authority, and (4) people who are ready for leadership.

Ideal leadership defines a leader as one who moves his or her organisation forward in a positive direction. Given the right conditions, combined with adequate capital, the result is favourable not only to the particular organisation, but also to the society at large.

While it is easy for every single business enterprise to quantify its own profits, who will want to quantify the profits of the society at large? I was studying the classic *'Dialogues of Plato'*, where Plato (427- 347 BC) brings out the concept that "our aim in founding the State was not the disproportionate happiness of any one class, but the greatest happiness of the whole". Similarly, during the same period, Tamil poet, Saint Thiruvalluvar, said, *"Pini inmai Selvam Vilaivinbam Emam, aniyenba Nattirku vainthu,"* that is, "The important elements that constitute a nation are: being disease free, wealth, high productivity, harmonious living and strong defence." We have to find how we can provide all these elements to all the citizens of the nation on an equitable basis for happiness. This will result in a peaceful world. What brings happiness to the human beings?

During the year 2003, I visited a Buddhist monastery at Tawang in Arunachal Pradesh for a day. I found that all the villagers were radiatingly happy in spite of severe winter cold aggravated by the altitude of the place. In the monastery, monks of all age groups were in a state of bliss, uncommon to the urban way of living. I wondered as to what was the unique feature of Tawang and surrounding villages which kept people at peace with themselves. The Abbot replied, "In the present world, we have a problem of distrust that has robbed people of their natural happiness and hence, they develop tendencies to behave violently. The moment you 'remove I and Me' from your mind, you will eliminate hatred towards fellow human beings. A mind bereft of hatred is immune to violent thoughts. If violence in our mind is taken away, peace descends, and it not only permeates into each cell of the body, giving us good health but also invigorates the ambience. Then, peace and peace alone will blossom in the society."

Like everything else in Nature man must learn to live in harmony within and without. The rise and fall in different times provides ample testimony of the futility of violent ways, both in thought and action. Mankind has been a witness to good leaders and bad leaders. Perhaps it takes both to evolve. In my opinion, all leaders can derive guidance from the speech of Abu Bakr, the First Caliph (632-634)—

> *I have been given the authority over you, and I am not the best of you. If I do well, help me; and if I do wrong, set me right. Sincere regard for truth is loyalty and disregard for truth is treachery. The weak amongst you shall be strong with me till I have secured his rights, if God will; and the strong amongst you shall be weak with me till I have wrested from him the*

rights of others, if God will. Obey me so long as I obey God and His Messenger. But if I disobey God and His Messenger, you owe me no obedience.[41]

By saying "If I disobey God and His Messenger, you owe me no obedience", Abu Bakr became the treble of heaven's harmony.

□

4

Living is Doing

"As the physical eyesight declines, the spiritual eyesight improves," said celebrated Greek philosopher, Plato (427-347 BC), in his later years. Einstein described a person, who only reads newspapers and books by contemporary authors, as an extremely myopic and yet scorns eyeglasses. What he meant was that one can't be completely dependent on the prejudices and fashions of his/her times. How will such a person ever get to see or hear anything else?

The key characteristics required for a societal transformer and entrepreneurs are desire, drive, discipline and determination.[42]

According to American novelist, Edith Wharton (1862-1937), in spite of illness or sorrow, one can remain alive long past the usual date of disintegration provided one remains unaffected by change.[43] Why should it be surprising that people who have carved out unique lives for themselves surrender to a monotonous end? Why should not they approach the end-phase of life creatively? You only hurt yourself when you're not expanding and growing. That's what evolution and the expansion of love are really about. None exemplifies it better than the lives of Marie Curie and Mother Teresa.

Marie Curie (1867-1934), Polish-French physicist and chemist, was a pioneer in the early field of radioactivity. Later, she went on to become the first two-time Nobel laureate and the only person with Nobel Prizes in two different fields of science. She got the 1903 Nobel Prize in Physics for discovering the radiation phenomena with Antoine Henri Becquerel (1852-1908) and husband, Pierre Curie (1859-1906). She got the 1911 Nobel Prize in Chemistry for her discovery of radium and polonium and her study of radium. Her daughter, Irene Joliot-Curie, continued working on the synthesis of new radioactive elements and won a Nobel Prize for Chemistry in 1935.

During the First World War, a global military conflict took place mostly in Europe between 1914 and 1918. Marie Curie designed the first mobile X-ray machine and travelled with it along the front lines examining soldiers for surgery. She was known to have an amazing memory and a diligent work ethic. She neglected even food and sleep while at work. She was known to have carried test tubes full of radioactive isotopes in her pocket. She stored them in her desk drawer, resulting in exposure to radiation. Marie Curie's death came from aplastic anaemia due to her massive exposure to radiation.

A similar zeal and determination emanated out of Mother Teresa (1910-1997). While Marie Curie died cradling nascent scientific ideas, Mother Teresa took the dying and cradled them. She persuaded Calcutta that leprosy was not contagious and got the leprosy-afflicted to build a self-supporting colony at Titagarh. Her biographer, Navin Chawla, writes that one of her happiest memories was of the man who said as he lay dying in her lap, "All my life I have lived like an animal on the streets and now I am dying like an angel." Her prized children, often without limbs or with terminal diseases, were whom she would rescue from dustbins.

From a single school which she started in a Calcutta slum in 1948; the Missionaries of Charity founded by her spread throughout the world. It rendered selfless service to the destitute and the needy. The Order provided in a year, food to half a million hungry children in five continents, treated a quarter of million sick, taught over 20,000 slum children and ran homes for the mentally destitute, the leprosy-afflicted, aids patients, the crippled and alcoholics and drug abusers. Her concern for the marginalised is unparalleled. She was awarded the Nobel Peace Prize in 1979.

Who will continue this great legacy? I feel science is already doing that. Empowered with science, thousands of human have raised themselves to angelic heights. Rightly applied, science is no less effective and palliative than the works of Madam Curie and Mother Teresa. Science is, indeed, a boon bestowed upon humanity. It has already affected fundamental changes in the ground rules of the world in favour of the underprivileged.

When I opted for Physics instead of Engineering in 1963, there was a pride associated with studying Physics. There is reduced status of the scientists in the society today primarily, because the students who cannot get through engineering schools alone are studying science. The trend has affected the quality of science in India. I find Sir C.V. Raman's (1888-1970) clarion call of indomitable spirit of greater relevance today.

> *I would like to tell the young men and women before me not to lose hope and courage. Success can only come to you by courageous devotion to the task lying in front of you. I can assert without fear of contradiction that the quality of the Indian mind is equal to the quality of any Teutonic, Nordic or Anglo-Saxon mind. What we lack is perhaps courage, what we lack is perhaps driving force which takes one anywhere. We have, I think, developed an inferiority complex. I think what is needed in India today is the destruction of that defeatist spirit. We need a spirit of victory, a spirit that will carry us to our rightful place under the sun, a spirit, which will recognise that we, as inheritors of a proud civilisation, are entitled to a rightful place on this planet.*

If that indomitable spirit were to arise, nothing can hold us from achieving our rightful destiny.[44]

Good teaching, indeed, emanates from research. The teachers' love for research and their experience in research are vital for the growth of institutions. Any University is judged by the level and extent of the research work it accomplishes. This sets in a regenerative cycle of excellence. Experience of research leads to quality teaching and quality teaching imparted to the young, in turn, enriches the research.

I am 75 now. When I reflect upon the work my peers and younger colleagues are doing, I can see four basic patterns—how they have dealt with changes in physical and cognitive capacities, in habits and personal traits, in relationships with the field, or in relationships with domains. It is only expected that a person's abilities to perform physically and mentally declines with age. Are there any positive changes?

Psychologists, particularly in the area of psychometrics[45], have long made a distinction between two broad types of mental activities. The first is what they call fluid intelligence, or the ability to respond rapidly, to have quick reaction times, to compute fast and accurately. This ability is measured by tests asking a person to remember a series of numbers or letters, recognise patterns embedded in more complex figures, or draw inferences from logical or visual relationships. This type of intelligence is supposedly innate and not affected by learning. Its various components peak early and there is a decrease over the years. Past seventy, the decline is usually significant.

The second type of mental ability is known as crystallised intelligence. It is more dependent on learning than on innate skills. It involves making sensible judgements, recognising similarities across different categories, using induction and logical reasoning. These abilities depend more on reflection than on quick reaction, and they usually increase with time, at least, till the age of sixty. I feel it is this kind of mental ability that improves or, at least, remains stable even in the ninth decade of life. I worked with Prime Minister, P.V. Narasimha Rao (1921-2004), and Prime Minister, Atal Bihari Vajpayee (b. 1924), and found them having this ability in abundance.

It was in 1993. I was appointed as the Vice-Chancellor of Madras University and I went to the office of Prime Minister Narasimha Rao on a farewell call with my predecessor and the then Scientific Advisor to the Prime Minister, V.S. Arunachalam. The sagacious Prime Minister kept looking at both of us and then asked me the reason of quitting my Defence R&D work. Covering the underlying dynamics, I cited my age of 62 years as a reason. Prime Minister Rao almost chided me saying that he was 80. He wrote on the file that I would continue as Chief of Defence R&D Organisation till further orders. No more words were spoken. I continued in service till 70.

Narasimha Rao, a multilingual, could speak 17

languages, including Urdu, Marathi, Hindi, Telugu and English with fluency akin to a native speaker. He also learnt several European languages including French and Spanish. Narasimha Rao became Prime Minister in 1991. There was acute economic stagnation. Prime Minister Rao believed India would benefit from undergoing an economic transformation. He invited renowned economist, Manmohan Singh, to become the Finance Minister to lead the reforms.

Prime Minister Rao provided the much needed political will and support to push economic reforms. India's economy grew by an average of about 6 per cent between 1991 and 2000. In a gesture quite unfamiliar in the partisan ways of Indian politics, Prime Minister Rao picked opposition leader, Atal Bihari Vajpayee, to represent India at the World Disarmament Conference. Prime Minister, Atal Bihari Vajpayee, continued the transformation and expansion of the national economy of the erstwhile government. I saw his decision-making ability during the Nuclear Tests in April 1998 and the Kargil War between May and July 1999. He has retained a position of esteem and respect amongst common people, seldom offered to politicians in India. I enjoyed working with Atalji in various capacities including discussing poetry.

People in their advanced years can accomplish certain things faster and better than before because of greater experience and better understanding. Older people have diminished anxiety over performance but are less driven.

On a personal level, I am probably more trustful in unconscious instincts than I was before and I'm not as rigid now. Perhaps, a reflection of this can be seen in the texture of the poems I write.

What we see in our mind's eye
Soon makes us cry.
So in the end only the journey.

Life itself teaches us so many things. As they grow, people learn from past mistakes and wrong decisions. This kind of learning can, indeed, be quite painful. Their absolute enthusiasm is tempered with by the realisation that they can be wrong. Here lies the biggest challenge for post-retirement people. The worst mistake people can make in their later years is that they become contemptuous of what is new. I am one of those who are open to change. Is there anything permanent in human affairs? We can lose physical energy and cognitive skills; we can lose the power and prestige of social position.

I see age in a positive light because I keep myself deeply involved in tasks that are exciting. In Rashtrapati Bhavan, I invested quite a bit of my time in creating a biodiversity park including a scientifically arranged herbal garden. Like the climber who reaches the top of the mountain and, after looking around in wonder at the magnificent view, rejoices at the sight of an even taller neighbouring peak, I am always prepared to pursue another exciting goal—the journey continues.

My profession and the challenge to my creativity almost always came from outside. For decades together, interesting and important issues kept arising and presented me with interesting opportunities for involvement. I always tried to make the most important task the one that I was working on. Arun Tiwari (b. 1955) pursued me for seven years to complete *Wings of Fire* as something more pressing would repeatedly cancel our writing-sessions. Later, when I took over as Principal Scientific Advisor to the Government of India, I tried to keep motivated by assigning a high priority to whatever it was that I was working on. *India Vision 2020* took shape during those years. Of course, I had Y.S. Rajan (b. 1943) working with me as the Scientific Secretary.

On the day I turned 70, I met Prime Minister, Atal Bihari Vajpayee, and sought his permission to retire from government service and go to Anna University to spend the rest of my life in an academic ambience. I had had a few achievements in the past, but those were over and done with and I was glad that I did well. How long could someone live by the past laurels? I hardly reminisced and dwelt on my past successes. I was visiting schools and meeting school children those days on my self-ordained mission of igniting young Indian minds and I wanted to focus my energies on this task.

Out of direct and operating employment, I shifted my focus on those factors that I thought would have greater leverage on the performance of young students, not only in the immediate academic years but also in their careers and overall lives. I started seeing learning as a life-long process. There must be something more for me to learn.

According to Danish-German psychologist, Erik Erikson (1902-1994), in a life-time, a person goes through eight psychological stages.[46] Each stage has a psychosocial crisis. In the first stage of infancy that lasts for about 1 year after birth, the psychosocial crisis is Trust vs. Mistrust. The child will let his/her mother out of sight without anxiety and rage, because she has become an inner certainty as well as an outer predictability. The balance of trust with mistrust depends largely on the quality of maternal relationship.

In younger years (1-3 years), the psychosocial crisis is Autonomy vs. Shame and doubt. Children in this age question, "Do I need help from others or not?" How the parents react to the child's newfound independence, indeed, draws the first contours of the child's personality. If the reactions are negative, the child may begin to feel shy forfeiting his/her natural and spontaneous behaviour. Doubt develops out of experiencing different behaviours from the same persons. The child gets baffled by seeing the front and back of the behaviour of adults around them. If the doubt is not resolved by the caring and attentive parent, it develops into outright fear psychosis called paranoia. These fears sometimes remain operational throughout life.

In early childhood (3-5 years), Initiative vs. Guilt crisis develops. Empowered with the ability to move and decide to perform certain things, the child develops guilt over the exuberant enjoyment of new locomotive and mental powers. The question of *how moral am I* arrives.

During 5-11 years, the question whether *I am good at what I do* arises. How a child does at school becomes important in development? It is usually Industry vs. Inferiority conflict. It is during these years that the child can become a conformist.

The adolescent is now concerned with how they appear to others. Ego identity is the accrued confidence that the inner sameness and continuity prepared in the past are matched by the sameness and continuity of one's meaning for others. These are the years (11-18 years) of Identity vs. Role Confusion.

In early adulthood (18-34 years), the new-found capacity for mutuality transcends childhood dependency. The grown-up child moves away from close relationships and shares with others. The danger at this stage is isolation which can lead to severe character problems. This phase of life is marked by a conflict of body and mind. Sixteenth century British poet, John Donne (1572-1631), wrote:

Your mind is slave to Fate, Chance, and king
O, desperate men,
And in your body poisons, weary,
And sickness dwell.[47]

Middle Adulthood (35-60 years) is marked by Generativity vs. Stagnation psychosocial crisis. Generativity is the concern in establishing and guiding the next generation. Simply having or wanting children doesn't achieve generativity. To generate means to do socially-valued work. The central task is creativity in this phase of life.

In later adulthood (60 years-Death), psychosocial crisis of ego integrity vs. despair dominates the psyche. Ego integrity is the ego's accumulated assurance of its capacity for order and meaning. Despair is signified by a fear of one's own death, as well as the loss of self-sufficiency, and of loved partners and friends. Healthy children, Erikson tells us, won't fear life if their elders have integrity enough not to fear death. The central task now is introspection. Handled well, it leads to a sense of fulfilment about life; a sense of unity with self and others. Wisdom settles in day-to-day activities. There is detached yet active concern with life in the face of death. The developmental task is to promote intellectual vigour; redirect energy to new roles and activities; and develop a point of view about death. British poet, Robert Grave (1927-1940), wrote:

> *Before our death, instead of when death comes, Facing the wide glare of the children's day, Facing the rose, the dark sky and the drums, We shall go mad, no doubt, and die that way.*[48]

What I understand from this is that if we live long enough and we resolve all the earlier tasks of adulthood—such as developing a viable identity, a close and satisfying intimacy, and if we succeed in passing on our genes by giving birth to a child and our values by rearing the child, then even a last remaining task is essential for our full development as a human being. This consists in bringing together a meaningful story of our past and present, and in reconciling ourselves with the approaching end of life.

Two important aspects emerge here. The first is about the individual life. A life is indeed a gift. No doubt, wavering, hesitation or fright must stop an individual from growing, performing and achieving all that is possible. British philosopher, Bertrand Russell (1872-1970), wrote, *"To teach how to live without certainty, and yet without being paralysed by hesitation, is perhaps the chief thing..."*

The second aspect is about social life. Every life is interconnected in a web of human relations and transactions. The web is much larger than it appears to the eye—family, friends, colleagues, community and so on. Any problem anywhere leads to mitosis. Harmony in the society is essential and it must be the axis of the education system. George Bernard Shaw (1856-1950) wrote:

> *The stability of a civilisation depends finally on the wisdom with which it distributes its wealth and allots its burdens of labour, and on the veracity of the instruction*

it provides for its children. We cram our children with lies, and punish anyone who tries to enlighten them.[49]

Albert Einstein took the argument of social inequality further. He wrote:

This crippling of individuals I consider the worst evil of capitalism. Our whole educational system suffers from this evil. An exaggerated competitive attitude is inculcated into the student, who is trained to worship acquisitive success as a preparation for his future career. The education of the individual, in addition to promoting his own innate abilities, would attempt to develop in him a sense of responsibility for his fellow men in place of the glorification of power and success in our present society.[50]

To me, education has two central functions relating to the individual and the society. The first is to educate the individual as a free individual—to understand and use critical thinking skills for determining the truth for themselves. The second is to educate the individual as a part of the society. We have a responsibility to contribute back to the society and environment.

Everyone must first give and then receive. This is ultimately why I began to study Physics and Philosophy, and why I have now read most of the great philosophers. I believe that Nature is being destroyed on this planet, and the truth is that this is very thoughtless and dangerous to humanity.

In April 2007, I visited Sree Siddaganga Math, Tumkur, Karnataka during the 100th birthday of His Holiness Sree Sree Shivakumara Swamiji. A message of 'Giving' came to my mind celebrating Swamiji's contribution:

It is in giving that we receive
For it is in giving that we share
And in sharing that we are happy
And our happiness stems from our care.
If you have knowledge, share.
If you have resources, distribute.
In the void of those who did not receive,
Contribute.

Have we not evolved from Nature and do we not depend on Nature for survival? This is not just the obvious concern of global warming and climate change, but the very food we eat, the air we breathe in, the water we need, all these things are produced by Nature. Humanity has evolved from the environment. Cycles of seasons, epidemics, diseases and so forth shaped the fittest of the species. The main cause of concern is the obvious fact that there are limits to our evolution as to how far we can change our environment before it begins to destroy us. The plethora of diseases already arrived out of neglect of environment and unnatural ways of living.

Unprecedented climatic changes are already adversely affecting. I wonder when man started drifting away from Nature. When was the genesis of this disconnection?

In September 2006, I visited Santhigiri Ayurveda Medical College in Kerala. A fourth year student, Gopalakrishnan, asked me if I saw deterioration in the age-old values and traditions of the society because of the common tendency of the masses to 'ape the West'. I answered: "The West, indeed, symbolises industrialisation. India must develop its industries. Agriculture alone cannot generate the wealth to give more than one billion people a certain quality of life. What we must not ape from the West is the 'I before you' way of thinking. Who will ensure this?"

The educational institutions must have a one-hour class every week to promote moral values and integrated living through reputed teachers. While I was studying in St. Joseph's College, Trichchirapalli, I remember the lectures given by the highest authority of the Jesuit institution, Rev. Father Rector Kalathil. Every week on Monday, he used to take class for an hour talking about good human beings, present and past, and what makes a decent human being. In this class, he used to give lectures on personalities such as the Buddha, Confucius, St. Augustine, Caliph Omar, Mahatma Gandhi, Einstein, Abraham Lincoln including some scientific personalities and moral stories linked to our civilisation heritage. It is essential in the secondary schools and colleges to arrange a lecture by a great teacher of the institution once a week for one hour on India's civilisation heritage and value systems derived from it.

If people in their later years look back with bewilderment and regret, they will be unable to accept the choices we have made. They will wish for another chance. Absence of proper education in their earlier life is the main reason. *A meaningful old age comes out of a meaningful life.* Old age, indeed, serves the need for that integrated heritage which gives indispensable perspective on the life cycle. I have seen in my father, who lived for 103 years, a detached yet active concern for life. He remains the wisest person of all the powerful and learned people I have ever met.

□

5

Flowering of the Mind

I was browsing the website of Geoff Haselhurst (b. 1959) which was created as a science forum of dynamic unity of reality.[52] Haselhurst sees two main problems of human nature. According to him, humankind is trapped in its collective mind; second, it is trapped in money. I can understand business people operating on the forces of the market. Interestingly, in the knowledge profession, there is an affinity towards conformity and prosperity. This makes it difficult for academicians and scientists to probe and explore new knowledge.

In history, any country revolves itself initially around a few stout and earnest knowledge giants.[51]

Human beings only sense a fraction of the real world, which is then represented by the mind. For example, in reality, the sky is not blue but a mere reflection. We see it blue because we see a certain frequency of light waves. Likewise, we 'see' things as separate and discrete objects although reason and physics tell us that all things in the universe are subtly interconnected. For example, the moon orbits the earth and the earth orbits the sun.

Classical Greek philosophers held that truth or falsity of a representation is determined solely by how it relates to objective reality. It was postulated that truth requires a proper fit of elements within a whole system. This led to the realisation that truth is constructed by social processes, which are historically and culturally specific: shaped through the power struggles within a community. However, it is argued that reference to the future is essential to a proper conception of the truth.[53]

Throughout the ages, sages advocated that we can't see what is true even when it is presented to us because what is true is not what we expect or want to hear. It is not that truth is not geared for us; we are not geared for that truth. In contemporary language, it is called choosing; choosing what is familiar or like most of us over what is different even if it is true or sacred. The intellectual arrogance of two great civilisations of India and China did not allow them to embrace the truth of industrialisation and technology for many decades. Of course, a deficit of political grit was also an issue. However, in the last two decades, both nations shed their fears of accepting the Western ways of generating wealth and recharted their course of development. The strength of India as a knowledge society and China as an industrial society has finally manifested.

In India, we have 5 million college level students, out of a total population of over 1 billion. By the American proportion, we would have 12 million or more in college. Our graduates have made an impressive mark abroad. Indians are the most visible foreign-nationality in many great institutions like NASA and companies like Microsoft. There is an enormous undeveloped hinterland with excess rural population without avenues for higher education. They land up in cities but never blossom as an individual. Peter Drucker (1909-2005) observed that India has done an amazing job of absorbing excess rural population into the cities. In fact, India's rural population has changed from 90 per cent to 54 per cent.[54]

The quality of our educational institutions, except for a prestigious few, is indeed a matter of concern. Also, talent is not attracted towards science as earlier. The last Nobel Prize in science came in 1983. There is a rush for acquiring information technology skills and getting jobs in the financially lucrative service sector. Is our youth really catching up with the world and is it prepared for the globalised economy of the twenty-first century? Is our education system on course?

The Indian education system is criticised for not meeting the aspirations of the society and for being unable to prepare people for the fundamental challenges of living.

Only children in rich and privileged families have access to good schools where commercial forces rule the roost. The education available to an average Indian child is grossly inappropriate for the requirements of a developed country in the making.

Padma Sarangapani[55] describes Indian youth as the *ajnatanvestas* or seekers of the unknown, as they stand now on the shores of the vast *brahmandam* of the third millennium. They boldly, yet humbly, seek to make sense of all the great happenings around them. To answer the dilemma that the Indian youth find themselves in, we seem to need educational insights that marry the most profound learning possible with every passing day; the subtle with the mundane; or to express it another way, the academic with the industrial and the theoretical with the practical.

India has produced great philosophers and teachers. I have read the works of Rabindranath Tagore (1861-1941), Swami Vivekananda (1863-1902), Sri Aurobindo Ghosh (1872-1950) and Jiddu Krishnamurti (1895-1986). I discussed extensively the works of Sir Syed Ahmed Khan (1817-1898) and Pandit Madan Mohan Malviya (1861-1946) who founded two great Universities at Aligarh and Benaras respectively. In the context of this book, the thoughts of Rabindranath Tagore and Jiddu Krishnamurti provide two polarities: Rabindranath Tagore viewed culture as the medium in which the individual potential finds expression; Krishnamurti saw culture as a barrier that must be overcome for innovation to happen. Between these two extreme positions, we find a spectrum of thoughts.

Krishnamurti started with the Theosophical Society as a young boy. His wake-up call came in 1925, after his brother's death.

> *An old dream is dead and a new one is being born, as a flower that pushes through the solid earth. A new vision is coming into being and a greater consciousness is being unfolded. ... A new strength, born of suffering, is pulsating in the veins and a new sympathy and understanding is being born of past suffering—a greater desire to see others suffer less, and, if they must suffer, to see that they bear it nobly and come out of it without too many scars. I have wept, but I do not want others to weep.*[56]

Although Krishnamurti's extensive work is subtle yet it is complex. He did not explicitly define positions; instead, his understanding is interwoven throughout his work. Krishnamurti saw human beings as having different facets (like intellects, emotions, appetites, bodies etc.). He said that none of the facets independently can define an individual. The facets are aspects of the whole. Humans have minds as well as brains, but they both deal with ideas about reality but not reality by itself. For example, we criticize corruption which is an idea. But we seldom hesitate in bribing our way through which is the reality of corruption.

The brain is the material centre of the nervous system and the organ of cognition. It is, therefore, responsible for the co-ordination of the senses, memory, rationality, intellectual knowledge, etc. The mind, which is not material, is related to insight, non-visual perception, compassion, and the profound intelligence that is the real goal of life. It is also the real goal of education. Obviously, one needs a brain that functions well, like one needs a heart or a liver that functions well. But the real source of acting rightly, of goodness, and of a virtuous life is the mind. In this unequal relationship between the brain and the mind, a good brain cannot ameliorate a mind except perhaps freeing itself from its conditioning and from activities that inhibit the mind's healthy functioning, such as hate, fear, pride, etc. Helping the brain do this is one of the main functions of education; not accumulating knowledge. It is to the full flowering of the mind that Krishnamurti felt education should direct itself.[57]

The human brain normally works by fragmenting the whole. One very important task that the brain needs to learn is to stop this fragmenting process when it is not necessary. Consequently, as possessors of both brains and minds, humans have the capacity of participating in the universe at different levels, from the specific to the general. For example, the reality of a flower is that it is a rose or a jasmine. Or, like a hard existentialist, one might consider most real that which is most particular. Here the specific fragrance of the rose defines the reality of the rose. Krishnamurti described human beings as not only having the capacity to venture to both limits but also to unite them.

Krishnamurti described education as a three-fold process.[58] (1) Education starts with addressing the elementary behaviour of the person; (2) the person is educated as an individual; and (3) the person is educated to be part of society, humanity, Nature etc. Education is, therefore, not limited to preparation for only a part of life, like work or career, but is about grounding oneself to understand the nuances of the life for a purposeful existence.

What could be the objectives of education? Surely, the schools and colleges must be centres of learning, a way of life which is not based either on pleasure or on self-centred activities, but on the understanding of correct action, the depth and beauty of relationship and the sacredness of a pious life.

Meaningful growth and real material change without unfortunate side-effects cannot be produced by just ensuring that young people acquire knowledge and skills, and teaching them to conform to the strictures and demands of society in order to get on in life. Merely to stuff the child with a lot of information, making him pass examinations, is the most unintelligent form of education. Educating a child to what he or she is not, is a crime.

Another concept that Krishnamurti stressed on, is freedom. But what is this freedom? Krishnamurti often stated that the purpose of education is to bring about freedom, love, the flowering of goodness and the complete transformation of society.[59] This freedom is, indeed, internal rather than the political type. Education must be concerned with deeper freedom of the psyche and the spirit. The inner liberation is both the means and the ends of education. There can be no freedom at the end of compulsion.

If you dominate a child and fit him/her into a template of one's fancy, are not its natural instincts being curbed? If we want education to bring about a true manifestation of a child's potential, there must obviously be freedom at the very beginning. It implies that both the parent and the teacher must be concerned with the natural development and not with how to help the child to become this or that. I was, indeed, sorry to learn that many children from affluent families are outsourcing their homework and assignments to poorer but brilliant children.

A transformed society will emerge only when education undergoes the process of transformation and liberation from cultural and social templates. Education is intended to assist people to become truly what they are. These intentions must not be just pleasant sounding ideals but practising norms in educational centres.

When the process of education is ingrained for inner liberation, both the students and the teachers interact on a level platform, not distorted by functional authority. In helping the student towards freedom, the educator is also changing his/her own values; and beginning to get rid of the 'me' and the 'mine'. This process of mutual education creates an altogether different relationship between the teacher and the student.[60]

The overriding quality of an educator, therefore, should be righteousness. Devoted solely to the freedom and integration of the individual, the right kind of educator must be deeply and truly righteous and bereft of any sectarian beliefs or rituals.

When we ask, "Who are you?" it is answered as, "I'm a doctor, an engineer, a businessman etc." though the question is asked about the 'being' the answer is a statement about 'doing'. Why this reversal or confusion? The importance of the students' 'being'—their deepest sensitivities, their goodness and intelligence, the depth of their questions about themselves and the world—must be central to any teaching methodology regardless of the career for which the teaching is done. Academic prowess, cultural abilities or capacities are not more important than the willingness and ability to lead a righteous life. In the final analysis, a student needs to be made known to his or her true self and not shaped by the teacher into this or that template.

Mind is infinite. It is everlastingly free. The real issue is the quality of our mind. Mind is the nature of the Universe which has its own order and its own immense energy. Indian tradition refers to the mind as *Chidakash* (consciousness space). The brain is the slave of knowledge and so is limited, finite and fragmentary. The brain can only become infinite if it frees itself from its conditioning. Then only there is no division between the mind and the brain. According to Krishnamurti, "Education is freedom from conditioning, from its vast accumulated knowledge as tradition." In the poignant words of American author, Ralph Waldo Emerson (1803-1882):

> *Go, speed the stars of Thought, On to their shining goals;—The sower scatters broad his seed, The wheat thou strew'st be souls.*[61]

This, however, does not undermine the academic disciplines which have their own important place in life. The point relates to precedence. Intellect is acquired through senses. The educational theories of Swiss philosopher, Rousseau (1712-1778); Swiss educationist, Pestalozzi (1746-1827); German educator, Frobel (1782-1852); and Italian doctor-teacher, Montessori (1870-1952)—all promote the idea that *sense must be educated before the intellect.* The traditional emphasis on the disciplining of the senses is weaning in our schools.

Freedom lies in understanding what you are from moment to moment. To understand life is to understand ourselves. Not only is a person's nature and deepest aspects to be uncovered, but each person also has a unique vocation that needs to be discovered. What he or she really loves to do have to be found and nurtured. Stereotyping children is a form of deprivation of the worst kind, especially if such deprivation is driven by vested interests of the governments, religion or social organisations.

In the recent times, the concept of capacity building has replaced the classical education model. Capacity building is an all-encompassing term for activities which strengthen the knowledge, abilities, skills and behaviour of individuals. Capacity building goes beyond an individual. It involves working on institutional structures and processes in the society.

United Nations Development Programme (UNDP) defined capacity building as the creation of an enabling environment with appropriate policy and legal frameworks; institutional development, including community participation, particularly of the women; human resources development and strengthening of managerial systems. It is a long-term, continuing process, in which not only students but also all other stakeholders such as industry, trade, community and government participate.

A good educational model is the need of the hour to ensure that the students grow to contribute to the economic growth of a nation. Can we sow the seeds of capacity-building amongst the students? There will be continuous innovation during the learning process. To realise this, special capacities are required to be built into our education system for nurturing the students. The capacities which are required to be built are research and enquiry, creativity and innovation, use of high technology, entrepreneurial and moral leadership.

The management of knowledge is beyond the capacity of a single individual. The amount of information that we have around us is overwhelming. There will always be a need to balance the desire of inventors to protect their discoveries, and the incentives to which such protection gives rise, and the needs of the public, which benefits from wider access to knowledge, with a resulting increase in the pace of discovery and the lower prices that come from competition.

The management of knowledge, therefore, must move out of the realm of the individual and shift into the realm of the networked groups. The students must learn how to manage knowledge collectively. When information is networked, the power and utility of the information grows as square as stated by Metcalfe's law.[62] Information that is static does not grow. According to Nobel Laureate, Joseph Stiglitz (b. 1943), "Indeed, monopolisation may result in not only static inefficiency but also reduced innovation. A patent that covered all four wheeled cars – that would have granted Selden a monopoly on the automobile – would have left little room for Henry Ford's innovation of an affordable car."[63] In the new digital economy, information that is circulated creates innovation and contributes to national wealth.

All students in our colleges should learn to know how to use the latest technology for aiding their learning process. Digital illiteracy is indeed a sacrilege. Universities should equip themselves with adequate computing equipment, laboratory equipment and Internet facilities and provide an environment for the students to enhance their learning ability.

Will the technological revolution diminish the role of a teacher? I think that the role of the teacher can never be undermined. In fact, the teacher will become even more important and the whole world of education will become teacher-assisted. The best of the teachers will be tele-ported to every nook and corner of the world. Care Foundation and Netaji Subhas Open University have already demonstrated this in the field of nursing education.

Besides computer-assisted learning, the aptitude for entrepreneurship should be cultivated from the very beginning in the university environment itself. We must teach our students to take calculated risks for the sake of larger gain, but within the ethos of a good business. They should also cultivate a disposition to do things right. This capacity will enable them to take up challenging tasks later.

Moral leadership involves two aspects. First, it requires the ability to have compelling and powerful dreams or visions for human betterment. Moral leadership requires a disposition to do the right thing and influence others also to do the same.

If we instil into all our students these five capacities, we will produce Autonomous Learners, self-directed, self-controlled, lifelong learners who will have the capacity to both respect and question authority in an appropriate manner. These are the leaders who would work together as a self-organising network and transform any state as a prosperous state. These capacities will enable the students to meet the challenges of our national mission of transforming the nation into a developed country by 2020.

When the students graduate, approximately 10 per cent of them take up research or some specialisation. The remaining 90 per cent of the graduates look for jobs. Where are the jobs? The youth must be empowered with the spirit 'I can do it'. The education system should inspire the young to achieve this capacity. Graduates with such a prepared mind can definitely be able to assume the leadership of small enterprises with the assistance of venture capital provided by banks. This will enable the nation to have a number of employment generators rather than employment seekers.

Most of the young readers of this book are going to work with the integrated system of psychology and physiology of human beings. Raymond Kurzweil (b. 1948), a pioneer in the fields of Optical Character Recognition (OCR), text-to-speech synthesis, speech recognition technology and electronic keyboard instruments, called computers as *emergent spiritual machines*.[64] The World Wide Web will make a tremendous impact in the way we communicate and live. Most of the computers and accessories will be micro-sized, wearable and will have wireless communications with one another. Moderately priced PCs, capable of performing about a billion calculations per second today, will be able to perform about a trillion calculations per second within the next decade. By 2020, the computational ability of an ordinary PC will exceed the capability of the human brain. By 2030, the capability of a normal PC will be around a thousand times more. How is man going to retain its supremacy over the planet?

What distinguishes human beings from all the less advanced forms of life on the earth is that, having, at last, become conscious of the challenge of survival, we have consciously undertaken to shape our own future. This requires us to look ahead, even beyond the span of any single generation. Any living generation enjoys the fruits of the efforts of its forefathers. This places on it the responsibility of creating a better future for the coming generation. Are we doing that?

India purchases liquid petroleum fuel to meet transport needs of automobiles, trucks, trains and planes. We import about 70 per cent of the total oil consumed. Oil imports constitute the single largest item in the total annual import bill of the country. Hence, our economy is dangerously vulnerable to fluctuating global fuel prices. There have been over 20 such instances in the last 50 years where our economy was almost destabilised on account of fluctuations in the international oil prices. About 40 per cent of the export earnings are funnelled back into importing oil for domestic consumption. A sustained 5 per cent rise in the oil price over a year will slash our GDP growth rate by 0.25 per cent and raise the inflation rate by 0.6 per cent.

According to the International Energy Agency (IEA), the energy intensity of the Indian economy is nearly three times that of the developed countries. This means that for producing the same quantity of output, the consumption of energy in India is almost three times that of any developed country.

With the domestic demand for oil growing at the rate of about five per cent a year, India's dependence on imported oil is likely to become near total within the next four decades. What kind of secure economy are we handing over to our future generations?

In a world of growing oil-rivalry between nation States, India has to find its place in the global energy game. With the future of West Asia as a reliable crude supplier becoming uncertain India must buy oil from the countries in South Asian region, Central Asia, Russia, Africa and Latin America. It is not easy, but is imperative.

We also need to shed our inhibitions and invest in off-shore oilfields and energy projects in Vietnam, Algeria, Kazakhstan, Indonesia, Libya and Syria. There are energy assets in Nigeria, Chad, Angola, Ghana and Cameroon, Congo and Gabon. India must bid.

Oil has always been thought of as the traditional cause of conflict. Countries have squabbled over borders in the hope that ownership of certain areas or tracts might give them access to new riches. However in the 21st century world, most international borders have been set, oil fields mapped and reserves accurately estimated. Humankind is now poised to fight over the water resources. Water is taking over from oil as the likeliest cause of conflict.

Although all natural water resources are replenished through the natural hydrological cycle yet their renewal rate ranges from days to millennia. The average renewal rate for rivers is about 18 days, *i.e.* to renew every drop taken out. While for large lakes and deep aquifer, they can span thousand years. Generally, a country with less than 1,700 cubic metre per capita is regarded as experiencing water stress, while less than 1000 cubic metre is regarded as water shortage.

India was ranked 100th among the 147 'water-poorest' countries in the world in a 'water poverty index' at the University of Keel and Institute of Hydrology at Wallingford.

Nothing short of a comprehensive long-term quest integrating all branches of human knowledge will be enough to grasp the finite reality of the earth where biotic and abiotic life are inevitably linked. Although science may superficially seem very different from philosophy, history, justice and aesthetics yet they all are components of a single continuous spectrum. Thus, India's water crisis demands for its resolution by a synergy of all disciplines of human knowledge.

Adapting to the earth's natural resource systems requires a very different set of complementary skills, knowledge and mindset. These systems are large, complex, interconnected. They cannot be precisely described or controlled. In managing these, the best available science has to be combined with an equal measure of thought and judgment based on human considerations.

According to T.N. Narasimhan[65], "Even as India is currently preoccupied with exercising its blessings of democracy, the Earth remains forgotten. Human values, however, noble, are transient. It is unrealistic to follow policies and enact laws assuming that Nature will be unaffected by the unprecedented promise of economic prosperity. India will do well to step back deliberately and reflect on whether this vision of prosperity based on materials and commerce can be sustained when the Earth remains ignored."

In India 2050, I can visualise water from the Brahmaputra and the Ganga systems flowing westwards to southern Uttar Pradesh, Haryana, Punjab and Rajasthan. Perhaps, it may eventually go southwards to the peninsular component connecting the Mahanadi, the Godavari, the Krishna, the Pennar and the Cauvery. Layered wells are constructed at the entry points of River Kosi flowing from Nepal and River Brahmaputra flowing from Tibet. These layered wells will store floodwater at different levels and will control the intensity of damage in low-lying areas by reducing the velocity of the flow. There are Nuclear Power Stations in every major State, an Indian Space Station, and above all, a conflict-free subcontinent. □

6

Nurturing a Garden

In November 2005, I visited Ajmer and prayed to Hazrat Khwaja Muinuddin Chishti (May the mercy of *Allah* be upon him!) at the Holy Shrine of Garib Nawaz (patron of the poor). Khwaja walked into Ajmer[67] at the age of 52 in 1190, on a divine mission, unique in the annals of Islam. He left his mortal frame at the age of 97. He brought the message of universal love and peace. He chose the way of non-compulsion in the true spirit of the Holy *Quran*, which says: "Let there be no compulsion in religion. Truth stands out clear from error; whoever rejects evil and believes in *Allah* has grasped the most trustworthy hand-hold that never breaks. And *Allah* hears and knows all things."[68]

See *the flower,*
How generously it
doles out
fragrance and
honey.
It gives to all,
gives freely its
essence.
When its work is
done, it falls
away quietly.
Try to be like the
flower,
unassuming
despite all its
qualities.[66]

Garib Nawaz provided a mystic interpretation of Islamic life within the bonds of religious orthodoxy. He maintained that a friend of God must have affection like the sun. When the sun rises, it is beneficial to all. All persons derive heat and light from it irrespective of whether they are the Muslims, the Christians or the Hindus. A friend of God must be generous like an ocean or a river. We all get water from the river to quench our thirst. No discrimination is made whether we are good or bad or whether we are related or strangers.

A friend of God is one who has the quality of hospitality like the earth. We are raised and cradled in its lap, and it is always spread below our feet. Mysticism is a practical spiritual discipline based on the insight of illuminated seekers after the truth. It is, in fact, a mission of higher religious order of any faith, which disdains strife and conflict in any form. Joy of self-realisation being the essence of religion is experienced after a long spiritual practice. The mystics discard the outward form of religion once they attain bliss. The concept of Sufism was, therefore, to focus the mystic power on the spiritual dimension of Islam with a view to shielding the believers from the outwardly and unrealistic dogma of faith.[69]

The Sufis have called the inner-being 'the child of the spiritual concepts', *tifl al-ma'ani* in Arabic. It is born from the heart, as the child is born from the mother. The ordinary child remains unstained by the manipulations of the world. This inner child is likewise pure and unstained by the heedlessness and physicality. Here 'child' symbolises purity. This 'child' is the real human being, as it is created by the Almighty God.

In Islamic parlance, heart is the abode of knowledge. The virtue of the heart is equanimity which is the quality of being calm and even-tempered. The fullness of the heart is marked by unbiased and unfettered evaluation of the reality. A wrong act is seen as wrong even if it is done by one's own blood relative. The metaphor of blind king Dhritrashtra in the epic *Mahabharata* depicts a blind heart.

The power to endure the reality is a greater virtue. In Islamic parlance, surrender to the reality of God belongs to the expansion of the breast. When Moses was sent to the court of Pharaoh, his immediate exclamation was "Expand for me my breast."[70]

When you are inspired by some great purpose for an extraordinary project, all your thoughts break the bonds; your mind transcends limitations; your consciousness expands and you find yourself in a great and wonderful world.

In February 2006, I addressed a gathering of more than two million people congregated at Jakkur Airfield, Bangalore. They came from more than 100 countries. They belonged to diverse religions and cultures. They were invited to The Art of Living Silver Jubilee Celebrations. The Art of Living movement founded by Sri Sri Ravi Shankar (b. 1956) has touched more than 20 million people worldwide. Sri Sri Ravi Shankar's key message is secularity of religion. He emphasises breath as the subtle link between body and mind, and many of his techniques use the breath as a tool to relax the mind. His *Sudarshan Kriya* technique involves cycle of breaths—long, medium and short. It claims to infuse the body with energy and harmonise the natural rhythms of the body, mind and emotions. What causes the dissonance of body, mind and emotions?

The term used for what one would like to be is persona. The persona of a person is how he/she or the family or the community wants him or her to be seen by the world. It is, indeed, psychological clothing which mediates between our true selves and our environment just as our physical clothing presents an image to those we meet. What we know consciously about ourselves is called ego. That part of us which we fail to see or know consciously is called *the shadow* by Swiss psychiatrist, Carl Jung (1875-1961). He described it as a psychic activity which continues independently of the conscious mind and is untouched, and perhaps untouchable by personal experience. The purpose of education is to bring light on to this shadow and integrate it into the conscious.

It is important to know how the shadow originates. We all are born whole. Let us hope we will die whole. But somewhere early on our way, we eat one of the wonderful fruits of the tree of knowledge, things separate into good and evil, and we begin the shadow-making process; we divide our lives. In the cultural process, we sort out our God-given characteristics into those that are acceptable to our society and those that have to be put away. This is wonderful and necessary, and there will be no civilised behaviour without this sorting out of good and evil. But the rejected and unacceptable characteristics do not go away; they only collect in the dark corners of our personality. When they have been hidden long enough, they take on a life of their own—the shadow life. Rumi has stated this so beautifully:

The angel is saved through knowledge,
The beast - through ignorance.
Between the two
struggle the people of this world.[71]

I have mentioned this in my book *Guiding Souls.* Many readers responded to this. Therefore, I chose to repeat it and elaborate here. The story goes like this: The Amir of Rum said to Rumi, "The non-believers used to worship and bow down to idols. Now we are doing the same thing. We go and bow down and wait upon the Mongols, and yet we consider ourselves the Muslims. We have many other idols in our heart too, such as greed, passion, temper and envy. We are obedient to all of them. So, we act in the very same way as the non-believers, both outwardly and inwardly, and yet we consider ourselves the Muslims!"

Rumi answered, "But here is something different; it enters your thoughts that this conduct is evil and utterly detestable. The eye of your heart has seen something incomparably greater that shows up this behaviour as vile and hideous. Brackish water shows its brackishness to one who has tasted sweet water, and things are made clear by their opposites."

Then, Rumi recited the above poem. There are three kinds of creatures. First, there are angels, who are pure spiritual conscience. Worship, service and the remembrance of God are their nature and their food. They eat and live upon that essence. Like fish in the water, their mattresses and pillows are the water. Angels are pure and free of lust. What favour do they gain by not yielding to such desires? Since they are free of these things, they have no struggle against them. If they obey God's will, it is not counted as obedience, for this is their nature, and they cannot be otherwise. Second, there are the beasts who are pure sensuality, having no spiritual conscience to restrain them. They, too, are under no burden of obligation. Finally, there remains the poor human being, who is a compound of spiritual conscience and sensuality. We are half angel, half beast, half snake and half fish. The fish draws us towards water, the snake towards the earth. We are engaged in a battle for ever. If our spiritual conscience overcomes our sensuality, we are higher than the angels. If our sensuality overcomes our spiritual conscience, we are lower than the beasts.[72]

What is the message? God has implanted in soul the light of faith to see these things as hideous. Confronted by beauty, this appears ugly. Yet others are not affected this way, they are perfectly happy in their existing state, saying, "This is absolutely fine." God will grant you your heart's desire—where your ambition is, that will be yours. As the bird flies with its wings, the believers fly with their aspirations.

The shadow is that which has not entered adequately into consciousness. It is the despised quarter of our being. It often has an energy potential nearly as great as that of our ego. If it accumulates more energy than our ego, it erupts as an overpowering rage or some indiscretion that slips past us; or we have a depression or an accident that seems to have its own purpose. The shadow that becomes autonomous is a terrible monster in our psychic house.[73]

The civilising process, which is the brightest achievement of humankind, consists of picking out those characteristics that are dangerous to the smooth functioning of our ideals. Anyone who does not go through this process remains 'primitive' and can have no place in a civilised society. We all are born whole but somehow the culture demands that we live out only part of our nature and refuse other parts of our inheritance. We divide the self into an ego and a shadow because our cultures insist that we behave in a particular manner. Perhaps, this is the legacy of man from having eaten the fruit of the tree of knowledge in the Garden of Eden as Christian theology puts it.[74]

Culture has been called the way of life for an entire society. As such, it includes code of manners, dress, language, religion, rituals, norms of behaviour and systems of belief. Culture takes away the simple human in us, but gives us more complex and sophisticated power. One can make a forceful argument that children should not be subject to this division too soon or they will be robbed of their childhood; they should be allowed to remain in the Garden of Eden till they are strong enough to stand the cultural process without being broken by it. This strength comes at different ages for different individuals and it requires a keen eye to know when children are prepared to adapt to the collective life of a society.[75]

It is interesting to travel around the world and see which characteristics various cultures affix to the ego and which to the shadow. It becomes clear that cultures are an artificially imposed structure, but an absolutely necessary one. We find that in one country, we drive on the right side of the road; in another, on the left side of the road.

In the Western world, a man may walk hand in hand with a woman in the street but not with another man; in India, he may walk hand in hand with a male friend but not with a woman. In the West, one shows respect by wearing shoes in formal or sacred places; in the East, it is a sign of disrespect to wear shoes when one is in a temple or house. In the Middle East, one burps at the end of a meal to show pleasure; in the West, this is considered as bad manners.

The sorting process is quite arbitrary. Individuality, for instance, is a great virtue in some societies and the greatest sin in others. In the Middle East, it is a virtue to be selfless. Students of a great master of painting or poetry will often sign their work with the name of their master rather than their own. In Western culture, one brings to his or her own name the highest publicity possible. The clash of these opposing points of view is dangerous as the rapidly expanding communication network of the modern world brings us closer together. The shadow of one culture is a tinderbox of trouble for another.[76]

It is also astonishing to find that some commendable characteristics turn up in the shadow. Generally, the ordinary, mundane characteristics are the norm. Anything less than this goes into the shadow. But anything better also goes into the shadow! Some of the pure gold of our personality is relegated to the shadow because it can find no place in the great levelling process, *i.e.* culture.

Curiously, people resist the noble aspects of their shadow more strenuously than they hide the dark sides. To draw the skeletons out of the closet is relatively easy, but to own the gold in the shadow is terrifying. It is more disrupting to find that you have a profound nobility of character than to find out you are a wastrel. Of course, you are both; but one does not discover these two elements at the same time. The gold is related to our higher calling, and this can be hard to accept at certain stages of life. Ignoring the gold can be as damaging as ignoring the dark side of the psyche, and some people may suffer a severe shock or illness before they learn how to let the gold out.[77]

Rabindranath Tagore (1861-1941), Asia's first Nobel Laureate, was of the belief that it is culture—the social environment, web of beautiful relations that brings this gold out. The shadow is lightened up and brought out in aesthetic art forms. The tremendous excitement and cultural richness of his family permitted young Rabindranath to absorb and learn subconsciously at his own pace, giving him a dynamic open model of education, which he, later, tried to recreate in his school at Shantiniketan. Rabindranath Tagore saw education as a vehicle for appreciating the richest aspects of other cultures, while maintaining one's own cultural specificity. He wrote:

> *Education has its only meaning and objects in freedom from ignorance about the laws of the universe, and freedom from passion and prejudice in our communication with the human world.* [78]

Rabindranath Tagore visualised an education that was deeply rooted in one's immediate surroundings but connected to the cultures of the wider world, predicated upon pleasurable learning and individualised to the personality of the child.

> *I invited thinkers and scholars from foreign lands to let our children know how easy it is to realise our common fellowship, when we deal with those who are*

great. It is the puny with their petty vanities that set up barriers between man and man.[78]

Rabindranath Tagore felt that a curriculum should revolve organically around Nature with classes held in the open air under the trees to provide for a spontaneous appreciation of the fluidity of Nature. In an essay entitled 'A Poet's School,' he emphasises the importance of an empathetic sense of interconnectedness with the surrounding world:

We have come to this world to accept it, not merely to know it. We may become powerful by knowledge, but we attain fullness by sympathy. The highest education is that which does not merely give us information but makes our life in harmony with all existence.[79]

Tagore's educational efforts were path-breaking. He was one of the first in India to argue for a humane educational system that was in touch with the environment and aimed at overall development of the personality. Shantiniketan became a model for vernacular instruction and the development of Bengali textbooks. It also offered one of the earliest co-educational programmes in South Asia.

One characteristic that sets Rabindranath's educational theory apart is his approach to education as a poet. It was this poetic vision that enabled him to fashion a scheme of education which was all inclusive, and to devise a unique programme for education in Nature and creative self-expression in a learning climate congenial to global cultural exchange.

In a poem that perhaps captures the essence of Rabindranath Tagore's goals for education, he writes:

Where the mind is without fear and the head is held
high,
Where knowledge is free;
Where the world has not been broken up into
fragments by narrow domestic walls;
Where words come out from the depth of truth;
Where tireless striving stretches its arms towards
perfection;
Where the clear stream of reason has not lost its
way into the dreary desert sand of dead habit;
Where the mind is led forward by thee into ever-
widening thought and action-into that heaven of
freedom, my Father,
Let my country awake.[80]

Rabindranath Tagore's contemporary litterateur and educationist, Roquiah Sakhawat Hossain (1880-1932), played a pioneering role in awakening Muslim women in Bengal. How can this phenomenon be described?

The contemporary term used is inclusive education. Basically, the idea is to address the learning needs of all children, youth and adults with a specific focus on those who are vulnerable to marginalisation and exclusion. It implies that all learners converge to a community education setting with an appropriate network of learning centric support service.

This is possible only in a flexible education system that assimilates the needs of a diverse range of learners and adapts itself to meet these needs. However, for it to happen, all stakeholders in the system, learners, parents, community, teachers, administrators and policy-makers, must be comfortable with diversity and see it as a challenge rather than a problem. The garden must have all kinds of flowers.

□

7

Specks in Brownian Motion

The management of knowledge must move out of the realm of the individual and shift into the realm of the networked groups.[81]

Faith-based giving has been deep-rooted in Indian culture. The concept of giving for charity was well established with individuals offering alms for ascetics. The main motivation behind the charitable acts has been the religious belief that a charitable activity leads to salvation. Ancient Hindu texts prescribed *Daana* (charity) as one of the ways to acquire merit and a place in heaven. In the Islamic tradition *sadaqah* (voluntary charity), *zakat* (obligatory charity) in addition to good treatment to orphans, parents and the elderly have been the forms of charity advocated. Since human beings receive God's mercy, serving

God regularly by means of good work and gift making is essential. In *gurudwaras* (Sikh temples), all those who visit are served free food (*langar*). Christian faith also discusses the notions of charity, which denotes the love between God and human beings. Love for human beings is considered as love for God. Surrender and contribution of a prescribed percentage of income as a measure of gratitude to God, were the common practices in Christian faith.

Voluntary action in India has sprung from a socio-religious background. The first half of the 19th century in Indian history showed the emergence and rise of social reform movements with the advent of British rule. Western ideas and the concepts of Christianity were introduced towards the end of the 18th century. The Charter of 1813 removed all restrictions on Christian missionaries in India and paved the way for the establishment and support of churches and Christian organisations in India.

In September 2004, I participated in the Sesqui-Centenary celebrations of St. George's College, Mussoorie. Standing majestically on a hill, a cut above the rest, this school was founded by Irish missionaries, Father Barry and Capuchin Friars in 1853. Society of the Brothers of St. Patrick has nurtured this school in the most praiseworthy manner. I asked Brother Dominic Jacob, "What propels selfless action?" I captured from the interaction that a stage comes in life when individuals take on responsibilities beyond their regular careers. Many successful people have created charitable institutions out of their life-time savings. What motivated them?

Scottish psychiatrist, Ronald David Laing (1927-1989), stressed the role of society, and particularly the family, in the development of an individual mind. He argued that individuals can often be put in impossible situations, where they are unable to conform to the conflicting expectations of their peers, leading to a 'lose-lose situation' and immense mental distress for the individuals concerned.[82] Opposite to this happens when the individual mind affects others around it and transforms multiple lives. These experienced individuals are like travellers who can return from the journey with important insights, and may even have become wiser and more grounded people as a result. They become creators of better and unprecedented lives.

When scientific organisations were being created in India, there was excitement everywhere. There were a chosen few—the visionaries, the likes of Homi Jehangir Bhabha (1909-1966), Vikram Sarabhai, Monkombu Sambasivan (M.S.) Swaminathan (b. 1925), Daulat Singh (D.S.) Kothari (1906-1993)—who were asked to create scientific organisations in the country. Then several young people were invited to take positions in the organisations that these visionaries conceived. Raja Ramanna (1925-2004), Satish Dhawan (1920-2002), Roddam Narsimha (b. 1933) and C.N.R. Rao (b. 1934) would have excelled anywhere, but they chose to work in Indian organisations.

These highly talented and committed scientists attracted talents from universities and industrial sectors. Thousands of them, have dedicated their lives to the great endeavours like putting a satellite into the earth's orbit, or creating nuclear electricity, or a ballistic missile system, or ushering in the green revolution, and now nurturing nanotechnology. Many other gifted people opted for administrative posts, became consultants and took up teaching jobs. The external pressure to diversify comes from the demands the environment places on the individual. There are many administrative positions in which a respected name is a great asset. Accomplished scientist, physicist, metallurgist, V.S. Arunachalam (b. 1935); and radiologist, Kakarla Subbarao (b. 1925) were also great administrators. Their leadership articulated on major public policy issues that have been engendered by a bureaucratic mindset.

There's so much beauty in science
that alliances with that is crude
collapse and perhaps and cease to be abstract
and become one with life
I dive into solitude again and there's no end
because without infinity nothing exists
so I persist.[83]

We are a developing nation. We are on our road to achieve better living conditions for our one billion-plus people. Science and technology will continue to advance.

It is evident that science and technology is directly linked to the generation of wealth. The modern world has stood witness to some of the major contributions as well as disasters because of science. Is science universal or is it that there is bad science and good science?

I believe that there is nothing like bad science or good science. Science is indeed universal. For example, we can either use nuclear science for producing electrical energy or use it for making a nuclear weapon. The choice lies with the user. The right type of use has to come from the right thinking. This thought led me to a deeper reflection.

Taken on its own, science is, essentially, a neutral commodity. It chooses no sides. The results of research remain neutral, till their ascribed meaning, or significance manifests through application. Truly controversial issues lie at the juncture of science and man. The new ways, that may have unanticipated moral or ethical implications, where safety or security risks are introduced, must be balanced against the benefits achieved.

I would like to cite here the example of societal implications of nanotechnology. I invited about 100 scientists and science administrators to Rashtrapati Bhavan on April 29, 2004. We deliberated one full day. There are concerns about existing and potential applications of nanotechnology. It is still unclear how it is possible to anticipate the consequences of nanotechnology development. Above all, it is yet to be seen how research and debate on societal and ethical concerns can be integrated into the research and development process.

Nanotechnology, which is the science of manipulating and characterising matter at atomic and molecular scales, and which integrates a multitude of science and engineering disciplines with widespread applications, warrants caution. My personal notion is that the convergence of information technology, biotechnology and nanotechnology can result in intelligent, self-replicating, nanoscale robots. Let me expand this thought process here because this concerns the careers of many young readers of this book.

There are two types of nanostructures: (1) Nanocomposites, nanostructured surfaces and nanocomponents (electronic, optical, sensors, etc.), something like 'fixed' nano-particles; and (2) 'free' nanoparticles. These free nanoparticles can be nanoscale species of elements, or simple compounds, but also complex compounds where, for instance, a nanoparticle of a particular element is coated with another substance, something like 'coated' nanoparticle or 'core-shell' nanoparticle.

One application of nanotechnology is the development of smart materials. This term refers to any material designed and engineered at the nanometer scale to perform a specific task. These materials can be designed to respond differently to various molecules. Such a capability can lead, for example, to intelligent drugs which will recognize and render inert specific viruses.

There are several potential entry routes for nanoparticles into the body. They can be inhaled, swallowed, absorbed through skin or be deliberately injected during medical procedures (or released from implants). Once within the body, they are highly mobile. How these nanoparticles behave inside the organism is one of the big issues that need to be resolved.

Is science (or technology) safe or dangerous? Do the benefits outweigh the risks? Are we as a nation in favour of or against a scientific and technological innovation? Should it be promoted? Can it be regulated? How can our answers to these questions protect mankind, and at the same time, enable science to move forward and provide life-enhancing discoveries we have come to expect and depend upon?

Shirley Ann Jackson[84] says, "Science presents a series of knife-edge issues—pros and cons, positives and potential negatives." Scientific solutions have not always meshed well with policy solutions. Is it not up to the science and engineering community, itself, to step forward and provide leadership? Let me comment upon what is close to my heart—nuclear science (and technology).

Three decades ago, France, a nation with a few coal and natural gas resources and virtually no oil resources, embraced a national nuclear power policy for generating its electricity. Today, more than 50 French nuclear power plants generate almost 80 per cent of that nation's electrical power and provide several billion dollars in annual revenues from sales of surplus power to other European nations. There has never been a nuclear power accident in France, and the nation safely reprocesses much of its nuclear waste. Since its nuclear energy produces no emissions, France has the lowest rate of carbon equivalent emissions. We took off in the nuclear electricity generation almost concurrently with France but faced various technology control regimes. However, decades of efforts braving those sanctions have eventually brought the United States to the negotiation table, opening doors for nuclear fuel for our power generation units.

Beyond power, nuclear by-product material is used in calibration sources, radiopharmaceuticals, bone mineral analysers, portable fluoroscopic imaging devices, brachytherapy sources and devices and gamma stereotactical surgery devices. Radioisotopes are used to identify drug-resistant strains of malaria, tuberculosis and other diseases; radiation is used in sterilising bone, skin and other tissues required for tissue grafts to heal serious injuries; and nuclear techniques are used to optimise malnutrition studies. Nuclear medicine is a speciality in almost all good Indian hospitals.

Agricultural productivity is enhanced by the development of new plant varieties through radiation-induced mutation. Researchers are working on using nuclear techniques to develop new plant strains adaptable to cultivation in saline lands. Isotope hydrology is used to map underground aquifers to improve groundwater management, as well as to investigate and recover from contamination events. We are in the game but need to develop further.

The societal, economic and 'quality of life' impact of scientific discoveries and technological innovations is very well-known today.[85] All developed countries, without exception, are strong in science and technology. What is happening in our science and technology institutions? The number of post-graduates in engineering and the physical sciences—and even in the computer sciences—are on the decline. Young talent is flocking to the booming information technology enabled services job market. How do we escape this quicksand?

In the past, we imported the science, engineering, and technological expertise we needed. All developing countries do that. The transition to a developed country must see indigenous innovation and capacity building in science and technology. We, undoubtedly, have immense talent that has not yet been channelled and harnessed. Young women and socially marginalised youth are yet to be initiated into science and mathematics. These groups offer India affirmative opportunity to construct the science and engineering workforce of the future.

Consider what it will take to do this: In about ten years (by the year 2015), our undergraduate population will expand by more than 10 million students. Five million of them will be students from these under-represented groups. Will this cohort want to study science and mathematics? What is going to spark and nurture their interest?

How do we ensure that they will be prepared, academically, to advance in science? If these young people have the desire and the preparation, will they have the means? Fewer than 10 per cent of youth in the lowest family income quartile go to college, compared with about 80 per cent of the top quartile income families. What are we doing to remedy this?

If these young people are willing, if they are prepared, and if they are financially able, then we will have bridged the science talent gap. Our challenge is to make this happen. The future scientific prowess of India depends upon closing the talent gap, which we can do only if we discover all the talent. But we shall have to take pains. It takes more than post-secondary education remediation strategies, or making 'merit-based decisions' about university admissibility. The fight cannot begin at the college classroom-door.

Moreover, educating for a livelihood is one goal. Educating for leadership is another. The leadership-oriented education empowers the individual with knowledge, not only of theories, but also of their mutual and true relations in life. All fields of study narrow as specialisation increases. The totally narrow view is myopic and ultimately faulty. The antidote is a basis in multidisciplinary approaches to problem-solving, and a broader education base.

No mafic rock is there on earth
Can hide the secret of its birth;
Where other methods try and fail.
Trace elements alone prevail.
My faith I place in my inheritance,
All other ground is sinking sand.[86]

There is a growing need for scientists to communicate. As complexity grows, so does the need for scientists to collaborate and work in teams, where the need to understand, explain, persuade and emphasise pertains. A young scientist entering industry today spends much time explaining science to consumers, legislators, policy-makers, environmentalists, judges, lawyers and the media. There is a greater-than-ever need for scientists themselves to heighten respect for scientific and technological solutions, and to alleviate a cultural fear of science. Scientists must understand and be governed by the social consequences of their work. Society will also need technologically knowledgeable, but broadly educated individuals in its public offices.

Scientists never claim absolute knowledge. Unlike a mathematical proof, a proven scientific theory is always open to revaluation, if new evidence is presented. Even the most basic and fundamental theories may turn out to be imperfect if new observations are inconsistent with them. Critical to this process is making every relevant aspect of research publicly available, which permits peer review of published results, and also allows ongoing review and repeating of experiments and observations by multiple researchers operating independently of one another. Transparency is the hallmark of a scientific temper.

In India, faith is held sacred. It is not very uncommon to see anecdotal claims about scientific impossibilities. Scientists are dared to debate over metaphysical issues. Science is reason-based analysis of sensation upon our awareness. As such, the scientific method cannot deduce anything about the realm of the reality that is beyond what is noticeable by already existing or theoretical means.

There is a principle of parsimony. All scientific theories are formulated and the most promising theory is selected after analysing the collected evidence. Some of the findings of science can be very counter-intuitive. Atomic theory, for example, implies that a granite boulder which appears as a heavy, hard, solid, grey object is actually a combination of subatomic particles with none of these properties, moving very rapidly in space where the mass is concentrated in a very small fraction of the total volume. Many of preconceived notions about the workings of the universe have been challenged by new scientific discoveries. Quantum mechanics, particularly, examines phenomena that seem to defy our most basic postulates about causality and fundamental understanding of the world around us.

Is there any goal of science? In my opinion, the underlying goal or purpose of science is to produce useful models of the reality for the individual and society. It is incorrect to say that science is totally evidence based. It is virtually impossible to make inferences from the human senses because their capabilities are severely limited. Humans cannot hear what bats can and cannot see what cats can. On the other hand, people can form hypotheses based on observations that they make in the world which is beyond any other specie.

By analysing a number of related hypotheses, scientists can thus theorise. These theories benefit society or human individuals who make use of them. For example, Newton's theory of Physics allows us to predict various physical interactions, from the collision of one moving billiard ball with another, to trajectories of space shuttles and satellites. Relativity can be used to calculate the effects of the sun's gravity on mass light-years away. The social science allows us to predict, of course, with limited accuracy at this point of time, things like economic forecasts.

Despite popular impressions of science, it is not the goal of science to answer all questions. The goal of sciences is to answer only those that pertain to perceived reality. Science does not and cannot produce absolute and unquestionable truth. Rather, science tests some aspect of the world and provides a reasonable theory to explain it.

Chemistry and biology together have transformed our ability to use and predict chemical and biological reactions and scenarios. A molecular scientist and Professor in the University of Tennessee, Rama Reddy Guntaka, has three decades of hands on experience in virology and molecular biology. He was a member of the team that discovered the proto-oncogenes for which it was awarded the 1989 Nobel Prize. He did the cloning and sequencing, for the first time, of the entire genome of Indian isolates of Hepatitis C Virus. Guntaka called a worldwide patent for Oligomers, which inhibit expression of Collagen Genes. This nucleic acid based drug is to control organ fibrosis in liver, kidney, lungs and heart. Guntaka invested significantly in setting up a laboratory in Hyderabad to do basic research in biotechnology.

While biotechnology is still in its nascent stage, other forms of technology have become so well-established that it is easy to forget the great scientific achievements that they represent. The refrigerator, for example, owes its existence to a discovery that liquids take in energy when they evaporate, a phenomenon known as latent heat. The principle of latent heat was first exploited in a practical way in 1876, and the refrigerator has played a major role in maintaining public health ever since. The first automobile, dating from the 1880s, made use of many advances in physics and engineering, including reliable ways of generating high-voltage sparks. The first computers emerged in the 1940s from simultaneous advances in Electronics and Mathematics.

Research in food technology has created new ways of preserving and flavouring what we eat. Research in industrial chemistry has created a vast range of plastics and other synthetic materials, which have thousands of uses at home and in industry. Synthetic materials are easily formed into complex shapes and can be used to make machines, electrical and automotive parts, scientific and industrial instruments, decorative objects, containers and many other items.

Along with these achievements, science has also brought about technology that helps save human life. The dialysis machine enables many people to survive kidney diseases that once proved fatal. Artificial valves allow sufferers of valvular heart disease to return to active living. Biochemical research is responsible for the antibiotics and vaccinations that protect us from infectious diseases, and for a wide range of other drugs used to combat specific health problems. As a result, most people on the planet now live longer and enjoy themselves healthier lives than ever before.

However, scientific discoveries also have a negative impact in human affairs. Industrial and agricultural chemicals pollute the environment. City air is contaminated by toxic gases from vehicular exhausts. The burning of fossil fuels such as coal, oil and natural gas releases into the atmosphere carbon dioxide and other substances known as greenhouse gases. These gases have altered the composition of the entire atmosphere, producing global warming and the prospect of major climatic changes in the years to come.

Here the metaphor of Brownian motion comes to my mind. Consider a large balloon of 10 metres in diameter. Imagine this large balloon in any widely crowded area. The balloon is so large that it lies on top of many members of the crowd. Since they are excited, each one hits the balloon at different times and in different directions with the motions being completely random. In the end, the balloon is pushed in random directions such that the movement is nullified. Assume that the force is exerted at a certain time. We might have 20 people pushing right, and 21 others pushing left, where each supporter is exerting equivalent amount of force. In this case, the forces exerted from the left side and the right side are imbalanced in favour of the left side; the balloon will move slightly to the left. This imbalance exists at all times, and it causes random motion. If we look at this situation from above, we see the large balloon as a small object animated by erratic movement.

Now return to Brown's pollen particle swimming randomly in water. A water molecule is about 1 nano metre, where the pollen particle is roughly 1 mirco metre in diameter, 1,000 times larger than a water molecule. So, the pollen particle can be considered as a very large balloon constantly being pushed by water molecules. The Brownian motion of particles in a liquid is due to the instantaneous imbalance in the force exerted by the small liquid molecules on the particle. The nation's balloon is moved in a similar way by the hundreds of thousands of people pushing it in thousands of organisations. What we see as the performance of the Indian nation is indeed the resultant performance of millions of organised efforts.

"There is no Indian science. Instead, Indian scientists are dealing with foreign science," feels Raj Reddy (b. 1937), the Mozah Bint Nasser University Professor of Computer Science and Robotics at Carnegie Mellon University. Raj Reddy told me that rural youth, even though they may be gifted and have high IQ, do not succeed in national competitive exams because most such exams require English, verbal, quantitative and analytical skills that they have never been taught. He is involved in setting up a 21st Century *Gurukulam* in Andhra Pradesh. It will be a postgraduate residential IT academy for gifted rural graduates. The big Indian balloon is too big to be meaningfully pushed by a few million *enthusiasts*. The giant of rural India must awake. The rural youth deserve a more different destiny than that of a peasant.

□

8

Education as a Spiritual Journey

Every citizen has a right to live with dignity; every citizen has a right to aspire for distinction. Availability of opportunities to resort to just and fair means is what democracy is all about.[87]

Every year on 5th September, India celebrates its teachers. The day is remembered as Teacher's Day to commemorate the birth anniversary of India's second President and teacher-philosopher, Sarvepalli Radhakrishnan (1888-1975). His dream was that "Teachers should be the best minds in the country." Distinguished teachers come to New Delhi and receive awards. I did the honours during my tenure as the President of India. Each time, I made it a point to interact with them and listen to their experiences. Many facts emerge from their polite but forthright accounts. I have come to know through them the pain experienced by many educators in the contemporary India.

One high school teacher from Maharashtra has highlighted the *pain of disconnection.* This disconnection is from colleagues, students and, above all, from his heart.

The culture, the size of the schools and attitudes of parents have changed so much that they appear strange, according to the teacher. There is an apparent emphasis upon achieving marks and gaining admission into 'prestigious' colleges. This pressure to 'achieve' has taken its toll on young minds and hence devastating the humane virtue of patience and gratitude. Optimism and collective commitment are getting scarce in our educational institutions. Intrusion of selfishness is evident. Some entrepreneurs see profits in education and hence reduce it to a mere service industry. This is not without grave social consequences.

I met fifteen spiritual leaders at Surat in October 2003 at the camp of Acharya Mahaprajna (b. 1920), the 10th Acharya of Terapanth. They belonged to various religions including Hinduism, Buddhism, Christianity, Islam and Sikhism. We released the Surat Spiritual Declaration.[88] The religious leaders were concerned that education in majority of schools, particularly in the small towns, is taming the young minds with dogma and obsolete concepts rather than empowering them with freedom of enquiry. Instead of allowing the buds of their spirits to blossom, the attempt is to dictate zealously the desirable outcomes of education in the life of the student. The Surat declaration was an attempt to safeguard young Indian minds from a spirituality of compliance. Spiritual tradition as a template, against which the ideas, beliefs and behaviour of the students are to be measured, is the last thing that must govern the education in our country of great cultural diversity. The idea 'to shape' the student to the 'template' by the time his or her formal education concludes is indeed ominous. Spirituality instead must form a vision of that which stands beyond, behind and within the passing flux of immediate things. Can we define spirituality to a young student without introducing his/her to religious terms?

First and foremost, it is important to know the distinction between spirituality in religion and spirituality as contrasting to religion. In recent years, spirituality in religion has often carried connotations of a believer having faith more personal, less dogmatic, more open to new ideas and myriad influences, and more pluralistic than the faiths of established religions. It also can connote the nature of a believer's personal relationship or connection with his/her God or belief system, as opposed to the general relationship with the deity understood to be shared by all members of that faith.[89]

I see spirituality as something which is real, to be explored by a close attention to our immediate world, and yet waiting to be realised. Spirituality is the capacity to dream, visualising something which is a remote prospect and yet the greatest of present possibilities of our life. I see spirituality as something which embeds us in harmonious relationships with others, and yet, at times, will require a journey in solitude. To me, a spiritual vision is one that makes us participants in the unfolding of the universe. Spirituality is, indeed, all about connectivity with the cosmos. It can be described as a vision requiring the exercise of mind, heart and body. A vision should be replete with consequences for any action.[90]

I feel spirituality is trust in the slow work of God. Young students are, quite naturally, impatient to reach the end without delay. They like to skip the intermediate stages; they are impatient of being on the way to something unknown, something new. I want them to understand that it is the law of all progress that it must pass through some stage of instability.

Young students must learn to let their dreams mature gradually—let them grow. Let them shape themselves, without undue haste. Don't try to force them on. Grace and circumstances acting on your own goodwill will certainly help you realise your dreams.

I have seen in my own life that those who spread their sails in the right way to the winds of the earth have always found themselves borne by a current towards the open seas. The more nobly a person wills and acts, the more avid he/she becomes for great and sublime aims to pursue. He/She is no longer content with family, country and the remunerative aspect of his/her work. He/She, indeed, wants wider organisations to create, new paths to tread, causes to uphold, truths to discover and ideals to cherish and defend.

Authentic spirituality wants to expose us to the truth—whatever truth may be and wherever it may take us. Such spirituality does not dictate where we must go, but trusts that any path walked on with integrity will take us to a place of knowledge. Such spirituality encourages us to welcome diversity and conflict, to tolerate ambiguity and to embrace paradox. By this understanding, the spirituality of education is not about dictating ends; it is about examining and clarifying the inner sources of teaching and learning. It is a process that rids us of the toxins that poison our hearts and minds.[91]

Rumi described the purpose of life "to know as we are known".[92] This is not easy today. The prevailing mode of knowing in education is rooted not only in fear but also in insecurity. It is creating disconnections between teachers, their subjects and their students. There is a need to look beyond knowledge inspired by a desire to control the surroundings and other people. The study of economics to dominate resources is knowledge as an end in itself. The study of applied sciences is a means to a practical end. There is another kind of knowledge that is open to us; the knowledge that originates in compassion or love. The profession of medicine and nursing thrives on this knowledge.

The goal of knowledge arising from love is bridging the individual that is separated out from the web of life around. Knowledge born of compassion aims not only at exploiting and manipulating the conditions but also at reconciling the world to itself. The mind motivated by compassion reaches out to know as the heart reaches out to love. Here, the act of knowing becomes an act of love. In such knowing, we know and are known as members of one community, *Vasudeiva Kutumbakam*, and this becomes a way of reweaving the bonds of community ensuring the safety and well-being of all, *Yogakshemam Vahamyaham.* [93]

An interesting concept of polarities elevated disconnection into an intellectual virtue.[94] Nobel Prize-winning Danish physicist, Niels Bohr (1885-1962), said, *"Opposite of a true statement is a false statement, but the opposite of a profound truth can be another profound truth."* If there is a day, there must be a night. If there is pleasure, there must be suffering. In certain circumstances, truth is not choosing between one or another but by embracing both. In certain circumstances, truth is a paradoxical joining of apparent opposites. If we want to know the truth, we must learn to embrace those opposites as one. The secular fabric of the Indian society is a living example of this truism.

To teach is to connect the individual with the reality. It, indeed, involves creating a bridging spiritual formation. Three spiritual practices are important: (1) the study of sacred texts, (2) the practice of prayer and contemplation, and (3) the community life. In Buddhism, it is so articulately said: *Buddham sharnam gachhami, Dharmam sharnam gachhami, Sangham sharnam gachhami* – to the Buddha I go, to good conduct I go, to community I go.[95]

The community indeed is a rich and complex network of relationships in which we must both speak and listen, and make claims on others, and make ourselves accountable. The cultivation of such communities of the truth should be our goal or objective as educators. A form of community that has the capacity to support authentic education must emerge among our teachers.

In September 2006, I visited Veeriya Vandayar Memorial Sri Pushpam College, Thanjavur. Veeriya Vandayar founded this institution fifty years ago in an interior region for providing the benefits of education to the rural masses. Three essential dimensions of a good educational campus come to my mind: openness, boundaries and an air of hospitality.

The educator and the participants work to clear away the clutter—whether those are meaningless words, pressure to get on with the daily round, obstructive feelings. The openness of a space is held by its boundaries. Learning can be painful if it is not structured. For this reason, hospitality is essential. Hospitality means receiving each other, our struggles, our newborn ideas, with openness and care. In a good classroom, truth is central. It is a place where every stranger and every strange utterance is welcome.

Learning spaces should invite people to speak truly

and honestly. People need to be able to express their thoughts and feelings. This involves building environments so that individuals may speak and where groups may gather and give voice to their concerns and passions. Learning spaces should honour people's experiences, give room to stories about everyday life. At the same time, we need to connect these stories with the larger picture. We need to be able to explore how our personal experiences fit in with those of others; and how they may relate to more general stories and understandings about life.

We cannot expect to reform education if we fail to cherish and challenge the human heart that is the source of good teaching. Good teaching is much more than technique. Good teaching, indeed, comes from the identity and integrity of the teacher. This means that they both know themselves, and that they are seeking to live life as well as they can. They are able to be in touch with themselves, with their students and their subjects—and act in ways that further flourishes the wholeness of the students.[96]

Teaching, like any other human activity, emerges from within. As I teach, I project the condition of my soul onto my students, my subjects and our way of being together. When I do not know myself, I cannot know who my students are. I will only see them through a dark glass of my ignorance, in the shadows of my unexamined life—and when I cannot see them clearly, I cannot teach them well. When I do not know myself, I cannot know my subject – especially at the deepest levels of embodied, personal meaning. I will know it only abstractly, from a distance, a congeries of concepts as far removed from the world as I am from personal truth. If we do not know who we are, then we cannot know those we work with, or the subjects we teach and explore.[97]

Many of us were called to teach by encountering not only a mentor, but also a particular field of study. We are drawn to a body of knowledge, because it shed light on our identity as well as on the world. *We did not merely find a subject to teach—the subject also found us.* Remaining open to that calling, listening for the voice of other subjects is vital if we are to sustain ourselves and our enthusiasm as educators.

Teaching is not a profession; it is a calling, a voice of moral demand that asks us to become someone we are not yet—someone different, someone better and someone just beyond our reach. A career in teaching is not for achievement but is a gift to be received. The voice of vocation is not 'out there' but within us calling me to be the person I was born to be, to fulfil the original selfhood given to me at birth by God. The authentic call to teach "comes from the voice of the teacher within, the voice that calls me to honour the nature of my true self."[98]

My friend G. Venkataraman, an accomplished teacher in his own right, narrates a story about C.V. Raman in his book *'The Big and the Small'*. Raman was in the first batch of Bharat Ratna Award winners. President Rajendra Prasad wrote to Raman inviting him to be his personal guest in Rashtrapati Bhavan. Raman regretted explaining that he was guiding a PhD student and that the thesis was positively due and the student was valiantly trying to wrap it all up. Raman felt that he had to be by the side of his student, to ensure that his thesis was completed. He signed the thesis as the Guide, and then had it submitted. He considered staying with his student as his duty and gave up the pomp of a glittering ceremony associated with the highest honour of the land.

What soil is to life on the earth, teachers are to society. Teachers, like soil, are the stage on which the human generations and other constructs of human knowledge are physically supported. Just as soil shelters seeds and provides physical support for their roots as they germinate, grow and mature into adult plants that create seed and thus perpetuate the cycle, teachers prepare and guide young minds to assume careers and become engines of growth and progress. Soil stores elements that, in the proper proportions and availability, act as nutrients for the plants growing in it. Similarly, teachers store and preserve tradition. Soil plays a central role in the decomposition of dead, organic matter. In doing so, not only it renders many harmless potential pathogens, including those affecting humans, but also adds to its store of potential nutrients. Likewise, teachers absorb the juvenile impulses and tame youthful beasts. Like soils of various kinds, acting in concert, are a critical factor in regulating the major elemental cycles of the earth—those of carbon, nitrogen and sulphur, some of which, such as carbon, play a vital role in the cycles of global climate, teachers sustain and refine culture. Just as the soil is the banquet table that feeds the multitudinous organisms living within and upon the earth—including humans, similarly, any society and its edifice is erected on good, noble efficient teachers.[99]

The earth is used as metaphor for the reality. The term reality, in its widest sense, includes everything that is, whether it is noticeable, comprehensible, or self-contradictory by science, philosophy, or any other system of analysis. Reality in this sense may include both being and nothingness. When two or more individuals agree upon the interpretation and experience of a particular event, a consensus about an event and its experience begins to be formed. This being common to a few individuals or a larger group, then becomes the 'truth' as seen and agreed upon by a certain set of people. Thus, one particular group may have a certain set of agreed truths, while another group might have a different set of truths that have reached consensus.

Different communities and societies have varied and extremely different notions of reality and truth of the external world. The religion and beliefs of people or communities are a fine example of this level of reality. Poetess Dorothy Walters writes:

No matter what you know,
someone is always wanting to correct you,
to sell you a list of goods,
from the shop marked 'authority'.
All the 'authorities' got
frozen into stone
years ago after the great flood
wiped out original knowledge,
and left behind only these granite shadows.
Reality is always soft clay,
ever shifting and changing its shape.
Fire it into form, and
at the very moment
you are hailing it as final truth
it will break in your hands.[100]

Like the human societies have been and are inextricably tied to the soil for reasons beyond measurable riches, for the historical wealth of the earth is archived in the soil, a wealth that nurtures cultures even as it sustains life, we need to conserve our teachers. Although we humans think of this wealth as 'raw materials' yet it is part of the atomic interchange in which each rock, microbe, butterfly, tree, drop of water, grain of sand and human being shares the ever journeying atoms of material creation. All of us, the successful, the creative, the virtuous, the resourceful people, were supported and nourished by our teachers. Let us go back to teaching before we leave this planet and become the manure to nourish the saplings of the future generations. Any society, that does not respect its teachers, eventually perishes.

I spoke to a wide cross-section of teachers to understand the struggles of a middle-class teacher working in a poor urban school. Four problems have emerged, namely low pay and prestige, distant and incompetent administration, students with social and economic problems and negligent or absent parents. In smaller cities, the problems of teachers have been compounded by general lowering of standards, social discrimination, increasing concerns about safety, infusion of money in getting into good schools and pressure to allot more marks and pass students on to the next class.

Today's students live in a world that is extremely fast-paced, constantly changing, increasingly culturally diverse, technologically driven and media-saturated. We cannot continue to deliver a 20th century, scientific-management, factory-model education. This new context of the 21st century requires that we redefine 'education', 'school', 'curriculum', 'teacher' and 'learner'. It requires that we provide an education designed to help our students truly succeed. I feel our education system needs to transform itself from a preaching to a coaching mode.

The onset of the third millennium of human history is a young and tender time, with much at stake. Yet, it may well prove to be another time of unprecedented opportunity for science and technology. Science, discovery and technological innovation alone can provide food, shelter, clothing, education, health and quality of life for all.

You see a smile on the faces of children when they are toddlers. They smile because they are blossoming innocently. When they come to their teens, the smiles slowly fade away and the signs of apprehension appear. When they complete their education, the top-most questions in their minds are, 'What would they do after their education? Will they get an employment?' The parents, who have spent all their savings on their children's education, also share the same concern. Concerns about employment are not only for those who are fortunate enough to have school and college education. It is the same fading away of the smiles, the shattering of the dreams and the weaning away of the gleam in the eyes that we see in every cross-section of youth in the country. The only answer to retain the smile from the child to the youth is to generate employment. It represents the aspirations and anxiety of nearly 540 million youth of India.

Unless India accelerates the process of societal transformation and raises its standard of governance and safeguards the sanctity of its public institutions, the possibility that ignorance and fear can interfere with—and even halt—its growth is not very remote. I personally believe that a scientific mindset guided by conscience, consensus, and by actions that take the complex values of our social and moral worlds into account is what we need to build at all levels of our system. We have but no choice. We have a lot of work to do. There is a great deal at stake.

□

Epilogue

To pen a foreword for Dr. Kalam's book, *'You are Born to Blossom'*, is a singular honour. It is a rare privilege to provide a commentary on the reflections of such a distinguished man: scholar, scientist, leader of India's space programme and the much-loved 11th President of the world's most populous democracy. It is also a considerable challenge, for any words of mine appear pedestrian and insignificant next to writing of such perspective and profundity.

Chapter headings such as *'The Wooing of Grain and Clay'*, *'The Treble of Heaven's Harmony'* and *'Specks in Brownian Motion'* give a flavour of the variety of the themes that he explores. Taking education, learning and teaching as the backdrop to his reflections, he writes about the human life-cycle, relationships within families, the significance of work, attributes of leadership, the nature of science, spirituality and moral choices. In exploring these themes, he demonstrates an erudite and loving familiarity not only with India's rich corpus of classical and modern writings, but also with thinkers and authors from all the cultures of the world over.

It is also a personal book that recalls many of the

steps in Dr. Kalam's own emotional, moral and intellectual development in ways that are certain to plunge readers into recollections of the people and institutions that helped them blossom. By reading this book, I was transported to the memories of my mother reciting poetry and to the book written by my grandfather who was a self-taught man of modest background. He wrote a book about Scottish essayist, Thomas Carlyle (1795-1881) alongside his job in the Excise Department. He inculcated in me love for mathematics.

Chapter 2 reminded me of Christ's Hospital, created as an orphanage for the City of London by Edward VI (1537-1553) and brilliantly fulfilling to date its mission to educate poor children. The school struck a beautiful balance between discipline and freedom.

In my later years, alongside my specialised formal studies of science and mathematics, I was able to explore three foreign languages, develop an appreciation of art and read widely.

Compared to this rich and stimulating secondary education, Oxford University, at first, seemed rather dull, but it, too, endowed me with lasting assets. Producing a weekly essay was the main vehicle for learning; a discipline that gave me a lifelong taste for writing. Paradoxically, this most collegial of universities also prepared the ground for my later love affair with distance learning. Oxford is indeed a seat of learning, not a place of teaching. Academics give lectures, certainly, but they are a marginal feature of the intellectual environment. The library, the essay and the tutorial are the route to learning. Study at Oxford is an effective distance education.

'You are born to blossom' opens up so many topics for reflection, poses so many practical challenges and asks so many profound questions that each reader will begin his/her unique intellectual journey. Coming, as I do, from a Western academic tradition, it is both challenging and exciting to read a work that moves so readily from analysis to synthesis; that emphasises both the collective and the individual; and that takes the Universe, no less, as the source of guidance for education.

The proper use of science and technological innovation for human purposes is a theme that runs through this work. The author notes that this is a time of unprecedented opportunity for science and technology because the world's population will double by the middle of this century. He argues that discovery and innovation can provide food, shelter, clothing, education, health and quality of life for all these people. He states:

"I dream that by 2020, schools in India will go from buildings to symbiotic nerve centres, with walls that are porous and transparent, connecting teachers, students and the community to the wealth of knowledge that exists in the world. The teacher will be orchestrating learning rather than dispensing information. Teachers would help students turn information into knowledge, and knowledge into wisdom. People of all ages will seek learning to prepare for life in the real world."

How can India's present reality be transformed into Dr. Kalam's dream? In my work at UNESCO and now at the Commonwealth of Learning, I have enjoyed familiarising myself with education in India. I find that the country already has in place most of the elements necessary to achieve the dream of its people. Indeed, the author urges Indians to have far greater confidence in their own achievements. Many of the policies and structures are already essayed. The challenge is to convert them into systems that bring teachers, learners and technology together in ways that are true to the high ideals of teaching and learning articulated in this ambitious book.

I refer, of course, to the EduSat satellite system, of which Dr. Kalam was one of the original architects, but equally to the arrangements for distance learning that India is putting in place at both school and university levels. Distance learning is a dry term that sounds like a behaviourist parody of the rich environments for learning that are described in this book. But beneath the dusty term lies a revolutionary reality that can be a vehicle for many of the reforms necessary to realise the dream.

India has created, through policies, technologies and institutions such as its open universities and open schools, the ingredients for making the paradigm shift that Dr. Kalam calls for. Now it needs people of vision and inspiration to blend the ingredients together. His book will nurture their vision and their inspiration.

Distance learning shares its first revolutionary feature with other applications of technology to the manufacture of products and the provision of services. Using various media, from print to the web, high-quality learning materials can be developed with low-unit costs. This makes education more accessible and more affordable. Open universities bring together teams of academics and experts to develop their courses, a singular innovation that converts teaching, like research, into a collective endeavour. Academics benefit from the robust but constructive criticism of their teaching materials from fellow team members. Students benefit from exploring a variety of perspectives and are encouraged to reach their own conclusions.

However, as this book argues powerfully, learning requires a good teacher and a comprehensive learner centric material. Distance learning has also invented or rather recovered, since times. In effective distance learning systems, the tutor metaphorically walks along with the student, as in the passage from Camus that Dr. Kalam quotes with approval at the end of Chapter 1: *"Don't walk in front of me; I may not follow. Don't walk behind me; I may not lead. Just walk beside me and be my friend."*

An aspiration that runs through this book is that "people of all ages will seek learning". Some argue that it is only with the maturity of adulthood that people are able to work out the truth for themselves. The experience of open universities, in India and across the world, is that, by combining learning materials with tutors who accompany students with respect and humility, distance learning can provide an ideal environment for older people. During my years as a vice-chancellor, hundreds of students told me, often with deep emotion, how their tutor-friend had helped them achieve the confidence that comes from finding new truths. Only through study later in life had they realised that they were indeed *'born to blossom'*.

The successful open universities continue to proclaim idealism about learning and human growth that is increasingly rare in conventional education systems characterised by the 'pain of disconnection' of which Dr. Kalam speaks in Chapter 8. I am sure he will approve of the sentiments expressed by Lord Crowther, speaking as Chancellor at the inauguration of the British Open University a few days after the cosmonauts had returned from the first landing on the moon in 1969:

"What a happy chance it is that we start on this task, in this very week when the Universe has opened. The limits not only of explorable space, but also of human understanding, are infinitely wider than what we believed. I am reminded of Milton's description of an even greater return from Outer Space with mission accomplished. The Planets in their stations listening stood, while the bright Pomp ascended jubilant. 'Open ye everlasting gates,' they sang, 'Open ye heavens your living doors. Let in the great Creator, from his work returned; Magnificent, His six days work, a World.' "

Sir John Daniel
President, Commonwealth of Learning

Endnotes

Chapter 1

1. Address to the students of the University of Mauritius, Port Louis, on 13 March 2006. Mauritius is an island nation off the coast of Africa in the southwest Indian Ocean. The first Indian came to Mauritius in 1835. In the beginning of the 20th century, 200,000 to 300,000 Indians were in Mauritius. Mahatma Gandhi stayed in Mauritius for two weeks in 1901 when he was travelling to India from South Africa. Today, there are 800,000 to 900,000 people of Indian origin who have settled here since then.
2. Albert Einstein published in the *Annalen der Physik* journal in 1905 his work on Brownian motion, the photoelectric effect and special relativity. Only the work on the photoelectric effect was mentioned in the Nobel Prize given in 1921 where Einstein proposed the simple description of light quanta. The light quanta are now called photons. The Einstein theory of general relativity was still disputed.
3. The outermost part of the earth's interior is made up of two layers: the lithosphere comprising the crust and the solidified uppermost part of the mantle. Below the lithosphere lies the asthenosphere which comprises the inner viscous part of the mantle. The mantle behaves like a superheated and extremely viscous liquid. The lithosphere essentially floats on the asthenosphere. The lithosphere

has broken up into what are called tectonic plates—in the case of the earth, there are ten major and many minor plates. These plates move in relation to one another.

4. Dana Cook Grossman, *Seeing Life Whole,* Dartmouth Medicine, Dartmouth Medical School, Summer 2006. "Life is a learning process for which there is no wholly adequate preparation. Although liberal education isn't perfect yet it is the best preparation for life and its exigencies."
5. Watson, Peter, *Ideas: A History from Fire to Freud*, Phoenix, 2005. In Greece, India and China, more than 2,000 years ago, there were sceptics who doubted whether the categories of human thought could correctly represent the world, but the recognition that these categories change significantly over time is distinctly modern. Thanks to thinkers such as Vico and Herder, Hegel and Marx, Nietzsche and Foucault, the notion that ideas have a history is an integral part of the way we think today.
6. *La ilaha illa Huwa.* Holy Quran, Ghafir (The Forgiver) Verse 40 : 3. "Who forgives sin, accepts repentance, is strict in punishment, and has a long reach. There is no god but He. To Him is the final goal."
7. The *Kalama Sutra (Anguttara-Nikaya,* Vol. I). In this Sutra, Gautama Buddha passes through the village of Kesaputra and is greeted by the people who live there: the Kalamas. The Kalamas greet the Buddha and ask many wandering holy men and ascetics pass through the village, expounding their teachings and criticizing others, 'Whose teachings should they follow?' In response, the Buddha delivered a sutra that serves as an entry-point to Buddhist beliefs to those unconvinced by revelatory experiences.
8. Vergil was an ancient Roman poet. These lines are from *The Aeneid,* a Latin epic written by Virgil in the 1st century

BC. The epic tells the legendary story of Aeneas, akin to Indian hero Rama. Aeneas travelled to Italy where he became the ancestor of the Romans.

9. Faris, Nabih Amin (Translator), *The Book of Knowledge* by Imam al-Gazzali (RA), Idara Isha'at-e-Diniyat, 2005. Al-Gazzali is one of the most celebrated scholars in the history of Islamic thought. His 11th century book entitled "*The Incoherence of the Philosophers*" marks a major turn in Islamic epistemology. "All causal events and interactions are not the product of material conjunctions but rather the immediate and present will of God."
10. Atkins, John Alfred, *Arthur Koestler,* N. Spearman, 1956. "Einstein's space is no closer to reality than Van Gogh's sky. The glory of science is not in a truth more absolute than the truth of Bach or Tolstoy, but in the act of creation itself. The scientist's discoveries impose his own order on chaos, as the composer or painter imposes his; an order that always refers to limited aspects of reality, and is based on the observer's frame of reference, which differs from period to period as a nude by Rembrant differs from a nude by Edouard Manet."
11. Thomas B. Ward, Ronald A. Finke, Steven M. Smith, *Creativity and the Mind: Discovering the Genius Within,* Plenum, 1995. The Theory of Multiple Intelligences (MI) tells us that our intelligences are multifaceted. There are, at least, eight types of intelligences in us: Bodily-Kinesthetic, Interpersonal, Intrapersonal, Linguistic, Logical-Mathematical, Musical, Naturalist and Spatial. Each of us possesses all of these intelligences but to varying degrees. These intelligences do not work in isolation but in concert.
12. Patrick Kavanagh (1904-1967) was an Irish poet. These lines are from his poem 'The Seed and The Soil' included in *Selected Poems of Patrick Kavanagh,* edited by Antoinette

Quinn, Penguin Twentieth Century Classics, Penguin Books, 1996.

13. Lin Yutang, *The Wisdom of India,* Jaico Publishing House, 2005. "It is easy to see why the Chinese mind cannot develop a scientific method, for the scientific method, besides being analytical, always involves an amount of stupid drudgery, while the Chinese believe in flashes of commonsense and insight. And inductive reasoning, carried over to human relationships (in which the Chinese are primarily interested) often results in a form of stupidity not so rare in American universities. There are today doctorate dissertations in the inductive method which would make Bacon turn in his grave. No Chinese could possibly be stupid enough to write a dissertation on ice-cream, and after a series of careful observations, announce the staggering conclusion that 'the primary function of sugar (in the manufacture of ice-cream) is to sweeten it'; or after a methodical study in 'Time and Motion Comparison on Four Methods of Dishwashing' happily perceive that 'stooping and lifting are fatiguing'...."
14. Sylvain Ctti and Tom Healy, *The Well-Being of Nations,* Organisation for Economic Cooperation and Development (OECD), 2001. "Human and social capital can be of key importance in contributing to a wide range of positive outcomes, including higher income, life satisfaction and social cohesion."
15. Technology Vision 2020, Technology Information, Forecasting & Assessment Council, New Delhi, 1996. TIFAC had taken up the challenge of delivering a Technology Vision for India for 2020 to provide directions for national initiatives in Science & Technology and a strong basis for a policy framework not only for investment but also for the development of an integrated science and

technology policy. Five areas were identified, namely Value-addition in agriculture, education, health, connectivity, strategic industries. Later, Dr. Kalam added composite rural development plan PURA.

16. Marcus Aurelius, *Meditations,* Courier Dover Publications, 1997. Marcus Aurelius had been a Roman Emperor since 161 BC to his death. He was the last of the 'Five Good Emperors' who governed the Roman Empire from 96 BC to 180 BC, and is also considered one of the most important stoic philosophers. *Meditations,* written on campaign between 170 BC–180 BC, is still revered as a literary monument to a government of service and duty and has been praised for its "exquisite accent and its infinite tenderness".
17. Albert Camus, *The Stranger*, Matthew Ward (Translator), Vintage; Reissue edition, 1989. Camus was the second youngest recipient of the Nobel Prize for Literature (after Rudyard Kipling) when he received the award in 1957. Camus preferred persons to ideas. "*Now the only moral value is courage, which is useful here for judging the puppets and chatterboxes who pretend to speak in the name of the people...*"

Chapter 2

18. Convocation address at Nizam's Institute of Medical Sciences (NIMS), Hyderabad, on 26 November 2002. NIMS is a Medical University offering PG courses in 14 Specialities and runs a 1000-bed hospital with impressive 3:1 patient-doctor ratio. There are 150 faculty members.
19. Shunryu Suzuki, *Branching Streams Flow in the Darkness,* University of California Press, 1999. Shunryu Suzuki (1904-1971) was a Japanese Zen master of the Soto school, who played a major role in establishing Buddhism in America. "Our tendency is to be interested in something that is growing in the garden, not in the bare soil itself. But if

you want to have a good harvest, the most important thing is to make the soil rich and cultivate it well," he said.

20. Ecclesiastes 9 : 11. Ecclesiastes is a book of the Hebrew Bible. It reflects on the meaning of life and the best way of life. The work emphatically proclaims all the actions of man to be inherently futile and meaningless, as the lives of both wise and foolish men end in death. While wisdom for the enjoyment of an earthly life is promoted, no eternal meaning emerges. The book suggests that one should enjoy the simple pleasures of daily life, such as eating, drinking and enjoying in one's work, which are gifts from God.
21. William Butler Yeats (ed.), *A Book of Irish Verse,* Routledge, 2003. These lines are from *Four Ducks on a Pond* written by an Irish poet, William Allingham. Yeats was awarded the Nobel Prize in Literature in 1923.
22. Davidson Richard J. and Anne Harrington (Editors), *Visions of Compassion: Western Scientists and Tibetan Buddhists Examine Human Nature,* Oxford University Press, 2001.
23. Richard Maurice Bucke, *Cosmic Consciousness,* Kessinger Publishing, 1998. Canadian progressive psychiatrist, Maurice Bucke (1837-1902) suggests that heaven is actually a form of divine perception, validating his speculations on cosmic consciousness via his own mystical experience. Perhaps, it is this predisposition that caused Bucke to expound on the idea that 'cosmic' awakening comes mainly to the middle-aged.
24. Holy Quran; Verse 47 : 12. Verily, *Allah* will admit those who believe and do righteous deeds, to gardens beneath which rivers flow; while those who reject Allah, will enjoy (this world) and eat as cattle eat; and the fire will be their abode.

25. From poem *My Mentor* written by David Heimburg associated with Nichiren Buddhist Association of America. Nichiren Buddhism is a branch of Buddhism based on the teachings of the 13th century Japanese monk, Nichiren. Nichiren Buddhists believe that personal enlightenment can be achieved in this world within the practitioner's current lifetime.
26. Anguttara Nikaya V. 159, Udayi Sutra. *The Buddha and the five qualities of a Dharma teacher.* "The Dharma should be taught with the thought: I will speak not for the purpose of material reward."
27. Faris, Nabih Amin (Translator), *The Book of Knowledge* by Imam al-Gazzāli (RA), Idara Isha'at-e-Diniyat, 2005. "The guides for the road are the learned men, who are the heirs of the Prophet, but the times are void of them now and only the superficial are left; most of them have been lured by inequity and overcome by the Satan. Everyone was so wrapped up in his immediate fortune that he came to see good as evil and evil as good. As a result, the science of religion disappeared and the torch of the true faith was extinguished all over the world. They duped people into believing that there was no knowledge except such ordinanees of government as the judges use to settle disputes when the mob riots; or the type of argument which the vainglorious display in order to confuse and refute; or the elaborate and flowery language with which the preacher seeks to lure the common folk. They did this. Apart from these three, they could find no other ways to snare illegal profit and gain the riches of the world."
28. Hazrat Inayat Khan (1882-1927) was born in India. An accomplished veena player, he received his spiritual training from Mohammed Abu Hasana of the Chishti Sufi Order. Following the command of his teacher to go to the Western

world and to unite the East and the West through the magic of music, Inayat sailed for America in 1910. His teaching strongly emphasised the fundamental oneness of all religions. He was deeply concerned that many of the Western religious traditions had lost knowledge of the 'science of soul', and the prayer and meditation techniques necessary to develop higher consciousness in mankind.

29. Camille and Kabir Helminski, *Rumi: Jewels of Remembrance,* Threshold Books, 1996. These lines are from *Mathnawi III:* 1445-1449. "When we are dead, seek not our tomb in the earth, but find it in the hearts of men." "Do not build much, for I intend to have you in ruins. If you build two hundred houses in a manner that the bees do, I shall make you as homeless as a fly. If you are the mount Qaf in stability, I shall make you whirl like a milestone."

Chapter 3

30. Address at the second convocation of Dev Sanskriti Vishwavidyalaya, Haridwar, Uttarakhand, on December 9, 2006.
31. *The Complete Poems of Emily Dickinson.* By Emily Dickinson, Back Bay Books, 1976. Emily Dickinson is an archetypal American poetess. She lived an introverted and hermetic life. Dickinson's poems are lyrical. "I heard a fly buzz when I die / The Stillness in the Room / Was like the Stillness in the Air / Between the Heaves of Storm."
32. William Wordsworth, *The Works of William Wordsworth.* Contemporary Publishing Company; Reissue edition, 1998. These lines are from his poem, *Upon Westminster Bridge* written in 1802. Wordsworth showed the link between human experience and the natural world.
33. SLV-3 is the name of four-stage, solid-propellant launch vehicle with a payload capacity of less than 50 kg into a

low-earth orbit with a mean altitude of 600 km at an inclination of 47°. Following an initial failure, the SLV-3 successfully orbited three Rohini satellites in 1980, 1981 and 1983 respectively. The SLV-3 formed the basis of the ASLV (Advanced Space Launch Vehicle).

34. The Agni (Fire, one of the 5 elements of Nature) missile is an Intermediate Range Ballistic Missile (IRBM) developed by India. It is capable of carrying a conventional payload of 1000 kg (2,200 lb) or a nuclear warhead. It consists of one (short range) or two stages (intermediate range). It is rail and road mobile. It is powered by solid and/or liquid propellants. Later, Agni-II with a range of 2,000-2,500 km was developed as a part of the 'credible deterrence'. Agni-III was tested on July 9, 2006, but failed.

35. William A. Tiller, *Science and Human Transformation : Subtle Energies, Intentionality and Consciousness,* Pavior Publishing Co., 1997. William Tiller has been a professor in the Department of Materials Science and Engineering at Stanford University. William Tiller hypothesised how to use one's own intentionality to bring about beneficial changes in one's body. Such changes naturally lead to significant growth in the individual's consciousness.

36. Floyd Jerred, *Understand the True Self,* Trafford Publishing Co., 2005. "Most people fail to find the treasure hidden within because they get off course and become lost in the storm of life. It is wrong to think that misfortune comes from the East or the West; they originate within one's own mind."

37. William Wordsworth, *The Works of William Wordsworth*. Contemporary Publishing Company; Reissue edition, 1998. These lines are from his best-known poem, *I wandered lonely as a cloud* was first published 200 years ago. The poem made *daffodil* flowers famous all over the world.

38. Wislawa Szymborska, *Poems New and Collected: 1957-1997*, Harcourt, 1998. These lines are part of a Polish poem "Reality Demands."
39. The branch of philosophy that studies the nature and scope of knowledge is called Epistemology. It primarily addresses the following questions: "What is knowledge?", "How is knowledge acquired?" and "What do people know?" For something to count as knowledge, it must be true. Knowledge is, therefore, a justified true belief. No one would gain knowledge just by believing something that happened to be true; one must also have a good reason for doing so.
40. Torbert, William R., *The Power of Balance: Transforming Self, Society, and Scientific Inquiry,* Sage Publications, 1991.
41. Abdul Basit Ahmad, *Abu Bakr As-Siddiq (RA): The First Caliph of Islam,* Dar-us-Salam Publications, 2001.

Chapter 4

42. Address at the convocation of the Indian Institute of Social Welfare and Business Management, Kolkata, on December 6, 2006.
43. Singley, Carol J., *Edith Wharton: Matters of Mind and Spirit,* Cambridge University Press, 1998.
44. Venkataraman, G., *Journey into Light : Life and Science of C.V. Raman,* The Indian Academy of Sciences, 1989.
45. In psychometrics, fluid and crystallised intelligence (abbreviated g_f and g_c, respectively) are factors of intelligence test scores originally described by British-American psychologist, Raymond Cattell (1905-1998). Fluid intelligence is a simple, innate, general ability, which stays fairly constant throughout life. It includes such abilities as problem-solving, memory, learning and pattern recognition. Crystallised intelligence is usually described

as being dependent on learning, while fluid intelligence is independent of past experience.

46. Erikson, Erik H., *Identity and the Life Cycle,* W.W. Norton & Company; Reissue edition (1994).
47. John Donne (1572-1631) is considered to be the master of the conceit, an extended metaphor that combines two vastly unlike ideas into a single idea, often using imagery. One of the most famous of Donne's conceits is found in *A Valediction: Forbidding Mourning* where he compares two lovers who are separated to the two long arms of a pair of a compass. These lines are a part of his poem *Death Be Not Proud.*
48. Robert von Ranke Graves (1895-1985) was an iconoclast in his poetry. He attacked cherished beliefs. He held that love was the only true subject for poetry. Graves confined most of his poetry to short lyrics. These lines are a part of his poem *The Cool Web.*
49. Evans, T. F., *George Bernard Shaw*, Routledge, 2004. George Bernard Shaw was uniquely honoured with both a Nobel Prize (1925) for his contribution to literature and an Oscar (1938) for *Pygmalion.* He was a harsh critic of formal education. "Schools and schoolmasters, as we have them today, are not popular as places of education and teachers are but prisons and turnkeys respectively in which children are kept to prevent them disturbing and chaperoning their parents," he said.
50. Albert Einstein, *The World as I See It,* Citadel Press, 2006. "Is it advisable for one who is not an expert on economic and social issues to express views on the subject of socialism? I believe for a number of reasons that it is," he said.

Chapter 5

51. Address at the Nanyang Technological University (NTU), Singapore, on February 2, 2006. This University is a research-intensive university with globally acknowledged strength in science and engineering.
52. Geoff Haselhurst is a Natural Philosopher. He created an Open Encyclopedia on the Internet, The Most Simple Science Theory of Physical Reality, Philosophy, Physics and Metaphysics of Space & the Wave Structure of Matter (WSM). It includes material on philosophy, physics and metaphysics, from the ancient Greeks and Indians to modern Western philosophy and physics. *www.spaceandmotion.com.*
53. Richard Schantz, *What Is Truth?* Walter de Gruyter, 2002, "Truth is correspondence, truth is coherence, truth is pragmatical utility, truth is primitive unanalysed property, and truth is misquotation."
54. Brent Schlender, Peter Drucker Sets Us Straight (On jobs, debt, globalisation and recession), *Fortune Magazine,* October 12, 2003. Peter Drucker made famous the term *knowledge worker.* In the Knowledge Age, wealth is based upon the ownership of knowledge and the ability to use that knowledge to create or improve goods and services. Product improvements include cost, durability, suitability, timeliness of delivery and security.
55. Padma M. Sarangapani is an independent researcher of Bangalore. She authored *Constructing School Knowledge: An Ethnography of Learning in an Indian Village,* Sage Publications, 2003. Her comments quoted here are from her article *The Great Indian Tradition* in *Seminar,* September 2003. *Seminar* is a highly respected monthly symposium founded by Raj and Romesh Thaper in 1959. It is published from New Delhi.

56. Kuiper, A.J.G. Methorst, *Krishnamurti*, Kessinger Publishing Co., 2004.
57. Forbes, Scott H., *Jiddu Krishnamurti and His Insights into Education,* Holistic Education Conference, Toronto, Canada, 1997. Scott Forbes did his doctoral work at The University of Oxford. He wrote *Holistic Education : An Analysis of Its Ideas and Nature,* Foundation for Educational Renewal, 2003.
58. Krishnamurti, *On Education,* All India Press, 1974.
59. Jiddu Krishnamurti, David Bohm, *The Limits of Thought,* Routledge (UK), 1999. David Joseph Bohm (1917-1992) was an American-born quantum physicist. He worked on The Manhattan Project which succeeded in developing and detonating three nuclear weapons in 1945. As Bohm grew older, he became increasingly preoccupied with Eastern mysticism and parapsychology. Gary Zukav writes in *The Dancing Wu Li Masters* (1979), "If Bohm's physics, or one similar to it, should become the main thrust of physics in the future, the dances of the East and the West could blend in exquisite harmony. Do not be surprised if physics curricula of the twenty-first century include classes in meditation."
60. Wright, Andrew and Francis, Leslie J., Embodied Spirituality: The Place of Culture and Tradition in Contemporary Educational Discourse on Spirituality, *International Journal of Children's Spirituality,* Volume: 1, Number 2, 1997, Pages: 8-1.
61. Ralph Waldo Emerson, *Emerson's Essays,* Harper Perennial, 1981.
62. Metcalfe's law states that the value of a telecommunications network is proportional to the square of the number of users of the system (n^2). First formulated by Robert Melancton Metcalfe (b. 1946) in regard to the Ethernet,

Metcalfe's law explains many of the network effects of communication technologies and networks such as the Internet and the World Wide Web.

63. In 1895, George Baldwin Selden, a patent lawyer of Rochester, New York, obtained patent for all gasoline-powered automobiles. Henry Ford thought the Selden's patent preposterous. "Although all invention was a matter of evolution," he said, "yet Selden claimed genesis." The nascent Ford Motor Company fought the patent case against an industry worth millions of dollars. The gathering of evidence and actual court hearings took six years. Ford lost the original case in 1909; he appealed and won in 1911. His victory had wide implications for the industry, and the fight made Ford a popular hero.
64. Raymond Kurzweil, *The Age of Spiritual Machines : When Computers Exceed Human Intelligence,* Penguin, 2000.
65. T.N. Narasimhan is Professor Emeritus in the College of Engineering, and in the College of Natural Resources, University of California at Berkeley, USA. He has quoted her *from Aspirations and an Earth Forgotten*, In: *The Hindu*, May 16, 2007.

Chapter 6

66. Address at the 25th convocation of Sri Sathya Sai Institute of Higher Learning, Puttaparthi, Andhra Pradesh, on 22 November 2006.
67. Khwaja Muinuddin Chishti, R.A. was born in Sajistan, East Persia in 1138. In compliance with a spiritual command, he left Medina for India passing through Isfahan, Bokhara and Lahore. He arrived at the barren and desolate land of Rajputana which was ruled by Prithvi Raj Chauhan. He settled there by the side of a hill close to Ana Sagar Lake.
68. Holy Quran, Sura *Al-Baqara,* Verse 2 : 256.

69. Saiyied Athar Abbas Rizvi, *History of Sufism in India,* Volume 2, Munshiram Manoharlal, 1992.
70. *Qala rabbi ishrah lee sadree.* Holy Quran, Sura *Ta-Ha;* Verse 20 : 25.
71. Arberry, Arthur John (Translator), *Discourses of Rumi,* John Murray, 1961, pp. 89-90. Arberry (1905-1969) was a respected scholar of Arabic, Persian and Islamic studies. He was Head of the Department of Classics at Cairo University in Egypt and, later, Sir Thomas Adams, Professor of Arabic at Cambridge University from 1947 until his death in 1969. His translation of the Quran is widely held to be the best written by any non-Muslim scholar.
72. Arberry, Arthur John, *Legacy of Persia,* Oxford University Press, 1953. Persia is the western name for the Iranian plateau. The Persians assumed different identities over the years. The Azeris live in the north-western corner; the Kurds along the border to Turkey and Iran; the Lur live in central western Iran; south of the Lur live the Bakhtiari; the Persians live in the central and southern Iran; the Baloch live in south-eastern Iran, as well as in south-western Pakistan; the Pathans live in southern Afghanistan; the Tadchiks live in northern Afghanistan. The Uzbeks, the Turcomans and the Kygyzians live in north-eastern Afghanistan. The Parsis mostly living in western India are descended from Persian Zoroastrian immigrants to the subcontinent.
73. Johnson, Robert A., *Owning Your Own Shadow: Understanding the Dark Side of the Psyche,* Harper, San Francisco; Reprint edition, 1993.
74. Barackman, Floyd H., *Practical Christian Theology: Examining the Great Doctrines of the Faith,* Kregel Publications, 2001.
75. Dan Sperber, *Explaining Culture : A Naturalistic Approach,*

Blackwell Publishers, 1996. Dan Sperber is a French social and cognitive scientist. He called culture "epidemiology of representations".

76. Johnson, Robert A., *Inner Work: Using Dreams and Creative Imagination for Personal Growth and Integration,* Harper, San Francisco; New edition, 1989. Robert Johnson is a gifted psychologist in the Jungian tradition. He studied at Sri Aurobindo Ashram in India. "I place my hope in individuals, not in the great collective swings. Nothing will see us through the age we're entering but high consciousness," he said.
77. Michael Balint, *The Doctor, His Patient and the Illness,* Elsevier Health Sciences, 2000. Michael Balint (1890-1970) was a psychoanalyst from Hungary, who emigrated to Britain in the 1930s. He worked to help develop a better understanding of the emotional content of the doctor-patient relationship. The Balint method consists of regular case discussion in small groups under the guidance of a qualified group leader. The work of the group involves both training and research.
78. Tagore, Rabindranath, Ideals of Education, *The Visva-Bharati Quarterly* (April-July), 1929.
79. Tagore, Rabindranath, Personality. London : Macmillan & Co., 1917, pp. 116-17.
80. Tagore Rabindranath, *Gitanjali,* Branden Books, 1979. Gitanjali (Bangla *Gitanjoli*) is a collection of 103 English poems, largely translations. While half the poems (52) in the English text were selected from the original Bengali volume published in 1910, others were taken from Noibeddo (1901), Khea (1906) and a handful from other works. A slender volume was published in 1913 with an exhilarating preface by WB Yeats. Rabindranath became the first non-European to win the Nobel Prize for literature.

Chapter 7

81. Convocation address Banaras Hindu University (BHU), Varanasi, on 2 March 2006. It was founded by Pandit Madan Mohan Malviya in 1916. It is a major Indian university located in Varanasi, Uttar Pradesh. It is reckoned as the largest residential university in Asia with a 1300 acre (5.5 sq. km) campus. The total enrolment in the University stands at just over 15,000.
82. Laing, David Laing, *Self and Others,* Penguin Books, 1990. He wrote extensively on mental illness and particularly the experience of psychosis. According to Laing, the strange behaviour and seemingly confused speech of people undergoing a psychotic episode were ultimately understandable as an attempt to communicate worries and concerns, often in situations where this was not possible or not permitted. Laing stressed the role of society, and particularly the family, in the development of madness.
83. These lines are from the poem *Fields* composed by Marco Mahler. These are taken from www. learnenglish.org.uk.
84. Nuclear Physicist, Shirley Ann Jackson, has been the 18th President of Rensselaer Polytechnic Institute, Troy, New York, USA. She served as Chairman of the U.S. Nuclear Regulatory Commission (NRC) from 1995-99. She spearheaded the formation of the International Nuclear Regulators Association (INRA) in May 1997.
85. Amartya Sen, Martha Nussbaum, *The Quality of Life,* Oxford University Press, 1993. "The concept of quality of life replaces incomes and utilities by the capability and human flourishing. The focus is kept on capability-building and not on indicators like per capita income."
86. Brenna Lorenz comes from State College, Pennsylvania, United States. These lines are from the website www.heptune.com that contains Science-related Humour.

Chapter 8

87. Convocation address National Academy of Legal Studies and Research University, Hyderabad, on 3 October 2003.
88. Surat Spiritual Declaration was signed on October 15, 2003, by Sri Balgangadharanatha Swamiji, Dr. Homi B. Dhalla, Bishop Dr. Thomas Dabre, Yuvacharya Mahashraman, Sadhvi Pramukha Kanakprabha, Jagadguru Sri Sri Sivaratri Desikendra Mahaswami ji, Rev. Stanislaus Fernandes, Swami Jitatmananda, Rev. Syed Muhammad Jilani Ashraf, Rev. Ezeikal Isaac Malekar, Prince Huzaifa Mohyiuddin, Brahma Kumari Sudesh Didi, Dr. Jaswant Singh Neki, Ven. Rahul Bodhi and by Maulana Wahiduddin Khan. It is available at the website of Jain Vishva Bharati Institute, Ladnun. www.herenow4u.de.
89. George F. Saint-Laurent, *Spirituality and World Religions : A Comparative Introduction,* McGraw-Hill, 1999.
90. Burkhardt, Margaret A, and mary Gail Nagai-Jacobson, Sprituality: Living Our Connectedness, Thomson Delmar Learning, 2001.
91. Richard Potter, *Authentic Spirituality,* Llewellyn Worldwide, 2004. Richard Potter experienced a wide cross-section of people and society. He worked for over 20 years with juvenile offenders and children in need of protection.
92. *Jalal Al-Din Rumi* (Original in Persian), Coleman Barks (Translator), Maypop Books, 1992.
93. Stephen Hetherington, *Good Knowledge, Bad Knowledge,* Oxford University Press, 2002. According to Stephen Hetherington, knowledge of a fact can be better or worse and in this way knowledge is never absolute. He argued in favour of non-absolutist way of conceiving of knowledge.
94. Daniel Patrick Liston, *Teaching, Learning and Loving: Reclaiming Passion in Educational Practice,* Routledge (UK), 2003.

95. Paul Williams, *Buddhism,* Routledge (UK), 2005. Bell Hooks, *Teaching Community,* Routledge (UK), 2003. Paul Williams is Professor of Indian religions at Bristol University and a leading scholar of Buddhism. He re-expressed Buddhism in Western language, symbols and archetypes.
96. Victoria Gill, *The Eleven Commandments of Good Teaching,* Corwin Press, 2001.
97. Turner, Edwin Arthur, *The Essentials of Good Teaching,* D.C. Heath & Co, 1920.
98. Toothman, Nelda C., *The Teacher Within,* Trafford Publishing, 2002.
99. David Hargreaves, *Creative Professionalism:* The Role of Teachers in the Knowledge Society, Demos, 1998. Professor David Hargreaves is Fellow of Wolfson College, Cambridge, UK. "If we are serious about creating an educational transformation in this country, then we all have to play a part in moving towards a high trust, innovative culture in which constructive partnerships flourish..."
100. Dorothy Walters, *Marrow of Flame: Poems of the Spiritual Journey*, Hohm Press, 2000.

□

Acknowledgements

This book germinated during my travels with Dr. Kalam to various centres of learning ranging from *panchayat* schools in heartland of India to world-renowned universities. I thank the members of Dr. Kalam's team, particularly, R. Swaminathan, H. Sheridon and R.K. Prasad. I was very well-looked after during all my tours with Dr. Kalam.

I received utmost support and encouragement from B. Soma Raju, Chairman of Care Hospitals and P. Krishnam Raju, Chairman of Care Foundation to devote my time and attention in working on this book. Sangma M.B., my pupil, assisted me in editing out the book and adding a fresh flavour to this book. I appreciate Namita for the cover design of this book.

I am thankful to my friends, notably, Rajiv Sangal, Director, International Institute of Information Technology, Hyderabad; Kasu Prasad Reddy, Chief of Maxivision Eye Hospital, Hyderabad; Priyesh Tiwari, Care Hospital, Hyderabad; S.G. Prasad, Care Foundation, Hyderabad; Dennis Marcus Mathew, *The Hindu*, now based at Alleppey, Kerala; and S.A. Taimiya, Frontline Publications, Hyderabad. They all have given me their valuable assistance.

My family—Anjana, Aseem and Amol—were co-operative and considerate as always. I feel proud of myself when I see my sons blossom in their respective careers in the IT Industry. They have shared thoughts and value-added concepts at large.

—Arun K. Tiwari

Index

A.R. Rahman 42
Abraham Joshua Heschel 42
Abu Bakr 67, 68, 158
Acharya Mahaprajna 135
Ajay Rathore 35
Albert Camus 32, 159
Albert Einstein 15, 82, 155, 165
Amelia Earhart 35
Amartya Sen 41
Antoine Henri Becquerel 70
Arthur Koestler 23
Atal Bihari Vajpayee 74, 75, 77

B.N. Prasad 62
B. Soma Raju 61
Baltasar Gracian 22
Benjamin Franklin 41
Bertrand Russell 81
Bill Gates 64
Brahm Prakash 43, 44, 54

C.H. Hardy 16
C.N.R. Rao 119
C.V. Raman 72, 142, 164
Clare Booth Luce 35
Carl Jung 107
Charles Darwin 16
Confucius 34

D.S. Kothari 119
Dorothy Walters 144, 173
David Joseph Bohm 167

Edith Wharton 69
Edward VI 150
Emily Dickinson 52, 162
Erik Erikson 78, 80

Father Felix 62
Floyd Jerred 163
Frobel 95

G. Madhavan Nair 55
G. Venkataraman 142
Galileo Galilei 16
Geoff Haselhurst 86
George Bernard Shaw 35, 81, 165
Giovanni Battista Vico 18

Hazrat Inayat Khan 49
Hazrat Khwaja Muinuddin Chishti 104, 168
Homi Jehangir Bhabha 119

Imam al-Gazzali 22, 46-48
Indira Gandhi 41
Irene Joliot-Curie 70
Isaac Newton 16
Iyadurai Solomon 43

James Watt 41
Jamshedji Tata 61
Jiddu Krishnamurti 10, 89, 167
John Donne 79, 165
Joseph Stiglitz 97

Kakarla Subbarao 120
Kabir 10
Kota Harinarayana 5

Leslie J. Walker 59
Lin Yutang 28, 158

M.R. Kurup 55
M.S. Subbulakshmi 38

M.S. Swaminathan 119
Madan Mohan Malviya 89
Mahatma Gandhi 29, 84, 155
Manmohan Singh 75
Maqbool Fida Hussain 41
Marcus Aurelius 30, 159
Marie Curie 70-72
Mark Twain 35
Montessori 95
Mother Teresa 70-72

Nicolaus Copernicus 11, 16
Niels Bohr 139

P.V. Narasimha Rao 74, 75
Padma Sarangapani 89, 166
Pestalozzi 95
Peter Drucker 88, 166
Plato 66, 69
Patrick Kavanagh 157

Rabindranath Tagore 10, 89, 113-15
Raj Reddy 133
Raja Ramanna 119
Ralph Waldo Emerson 34, 95, 167
Ramanujan 38
Rama Reddy Guntaka 130
Raymond Cattell 164
Raymond Kurzweil 99, 168
Rev. Fr. Ladislaus Chinnathurai 21
Rev. Father Rector Kalathil 84
Robert Frost 29
Robert Grave 80
Roddam Narsimha 119
Ronald David Laing 119
Roquiah Sakhawat Hossain 115
Rousseau 95
Rumi 172

S. Radhakrishnan 47, 134
Sarat Chandra Chattopadhyay 41
Satish Dhawan 54, 55, 119
Shirley Ann Jackson 123, 171
Shunryu Suzuki 159
Sigmund Freud 52
Sir Syed Ahmed Khan 89
Siva Subramanian Iyer 5, 40, 53
Sri Aurobindo 89
Sri Sri Ravi Shankar 106
Srinivas Ramanujan 16
Swami Vivekananda 10, 89
Sylvain Ctti 158

T.N. Narasimhan 103, 168
Thiruvalluvar 10, 66
Thomas Alva Edison 16
Thomas Carlyle 150
Tom Healy 158

V.S. Arunachalam 74, 120
Veeriya Vandayar 140
Verghese Kurien 61
Vikram Sarabhai 61, 119

William Butler Yeats 35, 160
William Harvey 16
William Szymborska 164
William Tillar 57
William Wordsworth 53, 57, 162-63
Wislawa Szymborska 58

Y.S. Rajan 77

Zohra 42

□□□